James McNair's CORN COOKBOOK

Photography by Patricia Brabant

Chronicle Books • San Francisco

Printed in Japan

Library of Congress
Cataloging-in-Publication Data
McNair, James K.
    James McNair's Corn Cookbook/
    Photography by Patricia Brabant.
    p. cm.
    ISBN 0-87701-645-3
    ISBN 0-87701-638-0 (pbk.)
    1. Cookery (Corn)
    I. Title
    II. Title: Corn cookbook
TX809.M2M39 1990
641.6'567—dc20   90-1776
                         CIP

Distributed in Canada by
Raincoast Books
112 East Third Avenue
Vancouver, British Columbia V5T 1C8

10 9 8 7 6 5 4 3 2 1

Chronicle Books
275 Fifth Street
San Francisco, California 94103

For Mary Val McCoy, the bravest woman I know, who adores corn as much as I do. With appreciation for her creative experimentation in the kitchen, her willingness to eat salad served from the floor or bread pudding when I forgot to add the butter, her steady encouragement and interest in my work, and her loving friendship.

Produced by The Rockpile Press, San Francisco and Lake Tahoe

Art direction, prop and food styling, and book design by James McNair

Editorial production assistance by Lin Cotton

Editorial and styling assistance by Ellen Berger-Quan

Photographic assistance by M. J. Murphy

Typography and mechanical production by Cleve Gallat and Charles N. Sublett of CTA Graphics

CONTENTS

Today about half of the world's corn is grown in the United States, making it the nation's largest money crop. Corn occupies one fourth of the country's total crop space, with Indiana, Illinois, Iowa, Michigan, Minnesota, Missouri, Nebraska, Ohio, and Wisconsin the major producers. About one fourth of the harvest is exported around the planet.

The vast majority of the United States corn harvest is used for livestock and poultry feed. Only 10 percent of the annual yield of this extremely versatile grain is reserved for humans. Of that portion, a large quantity goes to the wet corn processing industry, where the natural starchy heart of the kernels is extracted. This starch is turned into the corn syrups and corn sugar (dextrose) that are rapidly gaining ground on the sucrose that is traditionally used to sweeten many products. In turn, liquid dextrose is the source of the carbon dioxide gas found in carbonated drinks and refrigeration equipment, lead-free automobile ethanol fuel, and caramel coloring for countless food products, including whiskey and brandy. Wet milling also turns the germ of corn kernels into corn oil and into by-products used in livestock feed and human foodstuffs.

Dry millers distribute whole kernel corn, including the ever-popular popcorn, and produce cornmeal, grits, and corn flour. These products are sold on their own or further processed into breakfast cereals, snacks, pet foods, and myriad other foods and goods that range from blue jeans to insulation material.

Corn is also distilled into straight corn whiskey, or bourbon, which by law must be at least 51 percent corn.

Only a small percentage of the corn grown each year is eaten fresh, canned, or frozen, but for those of us who love its sweet flavor it is a major part of the overall corn picture. The recipes and general cooking tips that follow are divided into two sections: *FRESH* presents a number of ways to use sweet corn and *DRIED* includes some of my favorite dishes made from dried corn products.

NUTRITION

Corn is a good source of energy-sustaining complex carbohydrate and is very low in fat. Its protein is incomplete because only traces of some essential amino acids are present. When coupled with beans, seeds, nuts, or a little animal protein such as milk, butter, cheese, meat, poultry, or fish, corn protein is made complete.

Yellow corn strains contain high amounts of vitamin A (carotene); white corn has none. Both strains are rich in vitamins B and C and potassium. Small amounts of iron and other minerals are also present.

The gray tone of blue corn comes from it having a higher concentration of lysine, an essential amino acid, than what is found in other corn strains. Blue corn also has about 50 percent more iron, higher concentrations of several other minerals, and 20 percent more protein than yellow or white strains, which makes it softer and less starchy.

One unadorned medium-sized corn ear or ½ cup plain cooked kernels contains about 70 calories.

FRESH

For those of us who number sweet tender corn among life's grandest pleasures, it is difficult to imagine its being unknown to most of the world's population, before our century. It seems equally amazing that such a delicacy remains largely unappreciated by Europeans.

Fresh corn in yellow, white, or mixtures of the two should be harvested at its peak and cooked as soon as possible. Quick action is important because the natural sugar begins to convert to starch at the moment of harvest.

The sugar content of each corn hybrid determines its flavor. One cold January day I enjoyed some of the sweetest fresh corn I'd ever eaten, shipped into California from warmer environs. It was an example of the remarkable "supersweet" and "sugar-enhanced" hybrids that have been developed by corn breeders. These strains have double-sugar genes that help sustain the sugar content for a much longer period after the corn is picked; grow or purchase hybrids with such sweet-sounding names as 'Early Extra Sweet,' 'Florida Staysweet,' and 'Kandy Korn.'

The 1980s' obsession with tiny vegetables delivered baby corn on its edible cob to specialty produce markets. Previously its availability was limited to canned products from Asia.

An unsightly parasite, corn smut, sometimes grows over the kernels of ripening corn. Known as *huitlacoche,* maize mushroom, or Mexican truffle, this fungus has long been a prized delicacy south of the border. Thanks to the demand from Hispanic restaurants and food markets, some farmers in the United States have ceased eradicating this tasty pest and are selling the earthy-tasting fungus to the gourmet produce trade.

GROWING

This warm-weather crop requires a frost-free season of more than 140 days. As soon as the ground can be worked in the spring, prepare a sunny site with rich soil and good drainage. Dig down into the earth about a foot and work in a complete fertilizer. Plan on as many stalks as space permits; a minimum of a dozen is essential for pollination. As soon as frost danger is past, plant seeds about two inches deep, four to six seeds per foot, in rows about three feet apart; grouping several short rows provides better pollination than a single long row. For a long-running season, include several varieties that will mature at different times, or use the same variety but plant additional seeds every two or three weeks.

Thin seedlings to about twelve inches between plants; feed with liquid fertilizer when plants are about eight inches high and again when they reach about eighteen inches. Corn stalks like plenty of water; mulching will help retain valuable moisture.

BUYING

Purchase fresh corn as soon as possible after it is picked, preferably right from the farm. Look for true "sweet" corn; pass up the immature field corn that is sometimes sold. When locally grown corn is unavailable, opt for ears that have been kept on ice between the field and the market. Never buy corn that feels warm to the touch; it will probably cook up tough because heat, like time, activates starch conversion. Supersweet varieties, which hold their sugar content longer, are the best candidates for shipping and extended storage.

Stems and husks of fresh corn should be pale green, not straw-colored, and a bit moist. Avoid ears with brown stems.

STORING

Freshly picked corn should be used the same day. If corn must be kept for a couple of days before cooking, promptly store it with husks intact in the refrigerator.

When you must resort to ears that have been partially or completely husked, refrigerate them in open plastic bags.

Cooked corn may be refrigerated in airtight containers for up to three days.

To freeze fresh corn on the cob, drop husked and silked corn in simmering water and scald for four to eight minutes, depending upon size; do not boil. Immediately plunge corn into iced water until cool. Drain. Place in sealable freezer bags, pressing out as much air as possible. For whole kernels, scald the corn for only two or three minutes, drain, and cool. Cut off the kernels with a sharp knife and store kernels in airtight freezer bags or containers. Frozen corn keeps well for at least six months; thaw completely before cooking.

Fresh corn can be successfully canned. Because of corn's low acid content, it must be fully processed. Consult an authoritative book on canning for complete instructions and follow them closely.

PREPARING

To shuck corn, pull the husks down from the narrow end, then snap them off along with the stem. Twist silks at the top and pull off as many as possible, then complete removal with a dry vegetable brush or a plastic corn-silk brush. Cook corn as soon as possible after husking.

To cut kernels from cobs, rest the base of an ear of shucked, silked corn on a large, deep plate or inside a large bowl. With a sharp knife, cut down the length of the cob from the tip to the base. Leave behind a bit of the pulp to avoid mixing tough cob fibers into the corn. For most dishes, turn the knife blade over and scrape the cob with the blunt edge to remove pulp and milky juices. Two medium-sized ears of fresh corn yield about one cup corn kernels.

For creamed corn, run the knife blade down the center of each row of kernels the full length of the ear. Turn the knife blade over and with the blunt edge scrape the corn into the plate or bowl. Several passes over the cob may be necessary to release all the juices.

Mechanical corn scrapers make short order of removing corn from the cob. The best model slices off whole kernels with no extra pulp, plus it can be adjusted to cut kernels in half and scrape them off with pulp and juices. Check cookware stores and seed catalogs for this handy utensil.

HARVESTING

Corn is ready for harvest when the ends of the silks begin to dry and brown, about three weeks after silks first appear. When this happens, pull back the green husks and see if the kernels near the pointed tip of the ear are plump. Insert a fingernail into a kernel to check if it is juicy; with the exception of some supersweet varieties whose juice is always clear, ripe corn should exude milky liquid. Corn past its peak will have very little juice and will cook up tough.

To remove the ears from the stalk, pull them downward and twist them off.

For baby corn, harvest immature ears when they are about six inches long, before the kernels are fully developed.

To dry whole ears of corn, allow ears to remain on the stalks until the husks are browned and the kernels are hard, then pull them off the stalks. Strip the husks back but leave them attached. Tie the husks together with string and hang the ears in a warm, dry place until completely dried.

Corn on the Cob

Here are several ways to cook and season whole corn ears. At the height of summer, however, butter, salt, or other seasonings are really unnecessary.

To microwave corn, place unshucked ears in a single layer on a platter or directly on a carousel. Cook at full power until tender, about 7 minutes for 1 ear or about 12 minutes for 2 ears when cooking in a small microwave oven, or about 2 minutes for 1 ear and up to 14 minutes for 6 ears when cooking in a regular-sized microwave oven. With mitts or kitchen towel to prevent burning hands, remove ears from the oven and pull off husks and silks. Or, to serve ears in husks, pull husks back without breaking, pull off silks, and reform husks around ears.

To roast corn, choose ears with ends intact. Pull the husks back but leave attached at base; remove silks. Rub kernels with softened butter, if desired, and reposition husks. Tie narrow end together with a strip of torn husk or cotton string. Soak in water to cover for about 20 minutes; remove ears from water and pat dry with paper toweling. Grill over a moderate fire or roast in a preheated 375° F oven for about 15 to 20 minutes. Or, to roast shucked and silked corn, brush ears with melted butter or vegetable oil and place on a grill over a moderate fire for about 20 minutes or in a preheated 350° F oven for about 15 minutes.

To boil corn, shuck ears and remove silks. Fill a pot with enough water to cover corn when it is added; do not add salt, as it toughens corn. Bring water to a boil over high heat. Add the corn, cover, remove pot from the heat, and let stand for 5 minutes. Drain.

To steam corn, shuck ears and remove silks. Lay the corn on a rack set in a steamer over boiling water, cover pot tightly, and steam until done, about 4 minutes for young, tender corn, or up to 8 minutes for older ears.

Serve cooked corn immediately. Offer butter, salt, and pepper, or one of the flavored butters.

Serves 3 to 6.

6 ears fresh corn
Unsalted butter, softened or melted
Salt
Freshly ground black pepper

OPTIONAL
FLAVORED BUTTERS

Softened or melted unsalted butter seasoned to taste with ground dried hot chile, crushed Sichuan peppercorns, minced sage or other favorite fresh herb, or freshly squeezed lime or lemon juice.

Sautéed or Creamed Fresh Corn

8 medium-sized ears fresh corn
3 tablespoons unsalted butter
Salt
Freshly ground black pepper
1 cup heavy (whipping) cream
    (for creamed corn)

OPTIONAL ADDITIONS

½ cup chopped onion or sweet pepper
    (sauté until soft before adding
    corn)

About 3 tablespoons minced
    fresh herbs such as cilantro
    (coriander), mint, sage, or
    savory (add while sautéing)

3 cups cooked lima beans, drained
    (add with corn)

4 slices bacon, chopped
    (cook until crisp, drain, and
    reserve; sauté corn in
    3 tablespoons of the bacon
    drippings instead of butter; stir
    in bacon just before serving)

For the field-fresh flavor of corn on the cob without the mess at the table, sauté cut corn to serve as a side dish or to use in recipes calling for cooked corn. To cut calories, cook the corn in a little chicken stock or broth instead of the butter.

For creamed corn that's far superior to the canned product, add cream to sautéed corn and cook until the mixture is thickened and creamy. For less caloric creamed corn, dissolve four teaspoons cornstarch in one cup low-fat milk or low-fat evaporated milk and use in place of the cream. Serve creamed corn as an accompaniment, or use in recipes calling for creamed corn.

For sautéed corn, cut the kernels from the cobs as described on page 11; there should be about 4 cups.

For creamed corn, scrape corn from the cobs as described on page 11; there should be about 4 cups.

To sauté corn, melt the butter in a sauté pan or skillet over medium-low heat. Add the corn and sauté until tender, about 4 minutes for young corn, or up to 8 minutes for older corn. Season to taste with salt and pepper and serve immediately.

For creamed corn, stir the cream into the sautéed corn and cook until slightly thickened, about 10 minutes longer.

Makes about 4 cups; serves 4 to 6.

Corn Chowder

8 medium-sized ears fresh corn, or
    4 cups drained canned or
    thawed frozen corn kernels
6 ounces salt pork, diced, or 6 slices
    bacon, cut crosswise into 1-inch
    lengths
2 tablespoons safflower or other
    high-quality vegetable oil, if
    using salt pork
1½ cups finely chopped leeks,
    including pale green portion
2 cups chopped yellow onion
3 tablespoons all-purpose flour,
    preferably unbleached
4 cups homemade chicken stock or
    canned chicken broth
4 cups diced or sliced, peeled boiling
    potatoes (about 2 pounds)
1 tablespoon minced fresh thyme, or
    1 teaspoon crumbled dried
    thyme
2 bay leaves
1 cup heavy (whipping) cream
Salt
Freshly ground black or white pepper
Ground cayenne pepper or Tabasco
    or other red pepper sauce
Fresh thyme sprigs for garnish

Although this all-American favorite is best made with fresh corn, drained canned or thawed frozen corn kernels make an acceptable chowder.

If using fresh corn, cut the kernels from the cobs as described on page 11; there should be about 4 cups.

Transfer half of the fresh, canned, or frozen corn to a food processor or blender and purée until smooth. Return the puréed corn to the bowl with the remaining corn; reserve.

If using salt pork, place in a small saucepan, cover with water, and boil over high heat for 5 minutes to remove salt; drain. In a heavy pot, combine the salt pork and oil and cook until the pork is browned. If using bacon, cook until crisp. Add the leeks and onion and sauté until golden, about 15 minutes.

Stir the flour into the onion mixture and cook, stirring, about 2 minutes. Add the chicken stock or broth, potatoes, minced thyme, and bay leaves. Bring to a boil over medium-high heat. Reduce the heat to low, cover partially, and simmer until the potatoes are tender, about 30 minutes.

Stir the reserved corn into the soup and simmer 3 minutes longer. Stir in the cream and simmer until heated through, about 5 minutes longer. Season to taste with salt, pepper, and cayenne or pepper sauce. Ladle into bowls, garnish with thyme sprigs, and serve piping hot.

Serves 8 to 10 as a soup course, or 6 as a main course.

SEAFOOD VARIATIONS Substitute for chicken stock 4 cups homemade fish stock or 2 cups bottled clam juice combined with 2 cups water. Add with the cream about 3 dozen shucked small oysters, 4 dozen shucked steamed clams, 1 pound raw small bay scallops, 2 cups chopped cooked lobster meat, or 3 pounds firm fish fillets such as halibut, cod, or salmon, cut into large bite-sized chunks.

Corn, Cheese, and Chile Soup

6 ears fresh corn, or 3 cups drained
    canned or thawed frozen corn
    kernels
2 tablespoons unsalted butter
2 tablespoons corn or other high-
    quality vegetable oil
1 cup chopped yellow onion
2 teaspoons minced or pressed garlic
2 tablespoons all-purpose flour
1 cup finely chopped fresh, drained
    canned, or thawed frozen green
    mild to hot chiles
1 cup peeled, seeded, and finely
    chopped ripe or drained canned
    tomatoes
3 cups homemade chicken stock or
    canned broth
2 cups heavy (whipping) cream, or 1
    can (13 ounces) evaporated milk
12 ounces Velveeta or other processed
    cheese product or Monterey
    Jack or sharp Cheddar cheese,
    freshly shredded
Salt
Ground cayenne or other dried hot
    chile
Red chiles or red sweet peppers, cut
    into julienne or fanciful shapes,
    for garnish

For a smoother version of this rich, delicious soup, purée it in a food processor before stirring in the cream and cheese. Although I wouldn't normally suggest eating processed cheeses, these products, which are made from natural cheeses that have been melted and blended with emulsifiers, do make an exceptionally smooth soup. If instead you use a tastier natural cheese, be sure to melt it slowly and never allow the soup to approach a boil; also, this soup does not reheat well when made with natural cheese.

If using fresh corn, cut the kernels from the cobs as described on page 11; there should be about 3 cups. Reserve. If using canned or frozen corn, reserve.

Combine the butter and oil in a heavy saucepan and place over medium heat until the butter melts. Add the onion and sauté until soft but not browned, about 5 minutes. Stir in the garlic and sauté 1 minute longer. Add the flour and stir over medium heat for 2 minutes longer. Add the reserved corn, green chiles, tomatoes, and stock or broth. Bring to a boil, then reduce the heat to low and simmer, stirring occasionally, for about 15 minutes.

Stir the cream or evaporated milk and cheese into the soup and cook, stirring frequently, until the cheese melts, about 5 minutes; do not allow to boil. Season to taste with salt and ground chile. Ladle into bowls, garnish with red pepper, and serve immediately.

Serves 6 to 8 as a soup course.

Velvety Corn Soup

This Chinese classic is quick and easy.

Place 1 cup of the creamed corn and 1 cup of the stock or broth in a food processor or blender and purée until smooth. Transfer to a bowl and stir in the remaining corn and stock or broth. Reserve.

Heat the oil in a saucepan over medium-high heat. Add the minced onion, ginger, and ham and sauté for 1 minute. Add the sherry and cook until alcohol evaporates. Reduce heat to medium and stir in the reserved corn mixture. Bring almost to a boil, then reduce the heat to low, stir the cornstarch mixture until smooth, and add it to the soup. Cook, stirring constantly, until the soup is slightly thickened, about 1 minute. Season to taste with salt.

In a small bowl, beat the egg whites until frothy but not foamy. Transfer the egg whites to a small pitcher and drizzle them into the soup in a thin stream. Stir gently to distribute the egg threads.

Pour into a large bowl or tureen and garnish with julienned green onion. Ladle into individual bowls at the table.

Serves 6 as a soup course.

VARIATION Substitute ½ pound cooked crab or lobster meat, chopped, for the ham.

2 cups Creamed Fresh Corn (page 14), or 1 can (17 ounces) cream-style corn
4 cups homemade chicken or pork stock or canned chicken broth
2 tablespoons safflower or other high-quality vegetable oil
3 tablespoons minced green onion, white portion only
1 teaspoon minced fresh ginger root
⅓ cup slivered flavorful baked ham
2 tablespoons dry sherry
1 tablespoon cornstarch dissolved in 2 tablespoons cold water
Salt
2 egg whites
Green onion top, cut into 1-inch lengths and then julienned, for garnish

Corn Salad

Here is a simple recipe for a summer salad that can be altered according to what is on hand. The variations that follow present only some of the many possibilities. Cook the corn as described for Sautéed Fresh Corn (page 14) or by any of the methods explained in Corn on the Cob (page 13), or use leftover cooked corn. Drained canned or thawed frozen kernels make adequate substitutes for fresh corn.

In a medium-sized bowl, combine the corn, sweet pepper, green onion or chives, and basil or other herb; toss well. Stir in the mayonnaise and season with salt and pepper to taste.

Serves 6 to 8.

VARIATIONS Reduce the corn to 1½ cups. Add 1½ cups cooked rice or other grain or cooked white, black, or pinto beans.

Add diced fresh or canned green mild to hot chiles to taste.

Add ½ cup sliced or chopped green or oil-cured black olives.

Stir in a handful of crumbled blue, feta, or goat's milk cheese, or freshly grated Parmesan cheese.

Substitute about ½ cup of a favorite vinaigrette for the mayonnaise.

Sprinkle the finished salad with crumbled, crisply cooked bacon or cooked diced pancetta.

Add 1 cup bite-sized pieces of cooked seafood, poultry, or meat.

3 cups cooked corn kernels
(from 6 medium-sized ears),
at room temperature
½ cup diced red sweet pepper
¼ cup minced green onion, including
green tops, or fresh chives
¾ cup chopped fresh basil, cilantro
(coriander), or other favorite
herb, or a combination
1 cup homemade or high-quality
commercial mayonnaise, or to
taste
Salt
Freshly ground black pepper

Fresh Corn Tamales
(Tamales de Elote)

8 medium-sized ears fresh corn, with husks intact
2 tablespoons unsalted butter, melted
2 tablespoons high-quality pork lard, melted
1 tablespoon granulated sugar
½ teaspoon salt, or to taste
1 cup (about 4 ounces) freshly shredded sharp Cheddar or Monterey Jack cheese, or crumbled goat's milk cheese
¼ cup minced green onion, including green tops

At the height of fresh corn season, serve these flavorful tamales with a piquant tomato salsa. Some people call them "green corn" tamales, referring both to the Early American name for freshly picked corn and to the use of fresh green husks instead of dried ones for the wrappers.

Peel off the corn husks from the ears, being careful not to tear them. Cut off and discard the hard portion from the base end of the husks; reserve husks.

Remove silks from ears. Cut the kernels from the cobs as described on page 11; there should be about 4 cups corn.

Place the corn in a food processor or blender and chop finely. Transfer to a bowl and stir in the butter, lard, sugar, salt, cheese, and green onion.

Bring a large pot of water to a boil over high heat. Working with a few husks at a time, drop husks into boiling water and blanch briefly to soften. Remove husks from water and dry with paper toweling. Lay 1 large or overlap 2 medium-sized husks on a flat surface, smooth side up. Spoon about 3 tablespoons of the corn mixture onto the center of the husk. First fold one side of the husk over the corn mixture and then overlap with the other side. Fold one end up and over the top and then fold the other end up, overlapping the first end to form a square or rectangular package. Cut 2 long, thin strips from a blanched husk and tie the bundle with them, using 1 strip in each direction. Alternatively, bring the sides of the husk up and overlap them over the filling, then tie each end with a husk strip. Repeat with remaining filling and husks.

Line a steamer rack with extra husks. Stack the tamales, seam side down, on the husk-lined rack in up to 3 layers. Position rack over several inches of simmering water. Cover tightly and steam until centers are set, about 1 hour; unwrap a tamale to test for doneness. Serve warm.

Makes about 25 tamales; serves 6.

Baked Corn

12 medium-sized ears fresh corn,
  or 6 cups drained canned or
  thawed frozen corn kernels
6 eggs, well beaten
1 teaspoon salt
½ cup (1 stick) unsalted butter,
  melted

This simple preparation has been among my favorite recipes ever since my fifth grade teacher, Eula Cain, shared it with me many years ago.

Preheat an oven to 350° F. Butter an 8- by 12-inch baking dish, two 9-inch tart rings with removable bottoms, or eight 3-inch tart rings.

If using fresh corn, cut the kernels from the cobs as described on page 11; there should be about 6 cups. Combine the corn with the eggs, salt, and butter; mix well.

Pour the corn mixture into the baking dish(es) and bake until just set in the center when touched, about 30 to 40 minutes. Serve hot or at room temperature.

Serves 8.

Corn Pudding

A glorious use of sweet corn that goes wonderfully with grilled meats or fish.

Preheat an oven to 350° F. Grease a shallow 5- to 6-cup baking dish or six 6-ounce ramekins or other individual baking dishes.

If using fresh corn, cut the kernels from the cobs as described on page 11; there should be about 3 cups. Combine the corn with the cream, melted butter, egg yolks, nutmeg, salt, and pepper to taste; mix well.

In a separate bowl, beat the egg whites until stiff but not dry. Fold the egg whites into the corn mixture, then spoon the mixture into the prepared baking dish. Place the dish in a large pan and add hot water to pan to reach halfway up the sides of the dish(es). Bake until a knife inserted in the center comes out clean, about 30 to 40 minutes. Lightly cover with aluminum foil if tops begin to get too brown. If desired, run a dull knife blade around the rim of individual puddings, invert dishes, and turn out puddings. Serve immediately.

Serves 6.

VARIATIONS Before folding in egg whites, add ⅓ cup roasted, peeled, and finely chopped red sweet pepper to the corn mixture.

Before folding in egg whites, add ½ cup freshly shredded sharp Cheddar or other good-melting cheese to the corn mixture.

Before folding in egg whites, add 3 tablespoons minced fresh chives, chervil, savory, or other delicately flavored herb to the corn mixture.

For a lighter custard, reduce the corn to 2 cups (from about 4 ears).

For a spicy version, before folding in egg whites, season the corn mixture to taste with ground cayenne or other ground dried hot chile or Tabasco or other red pepper sauce. Alternatively, stir in 2 tablespoons chopped fresh or canned green hot chile.

6 medium-sized ears fresh corn,
   or 3 cups drained canned or
   thawed frozen corn kernels
1 cup heavy (whipping) cream
2 tablespoons unsalted butter, melted
3 large eggs, separated
⅛ teaspoon freshly grated nutmeg
1 teaspoon salt, or to taste
Freshly ground white pepper

Upside-Down Corn Cake

On balmy summer nights at Lake Tahoe, my southern roots are satisfied with a simple supper featuring this classic dish accompanied with a plate of sliced ripe tomatoes and some green beans or fried okra. Although I often prepare this down-home dish without hot peppers, they do contribute a bit of zing to the crisp-edged corn cake that forms in the smoking-hot skillet. Cook the cake in an iron or other heavy skillet; pans with nonstick coatings won't produce the essential crisp crust.

The cake is delicious plain or with fresh tomato salsa or a good tomato sauce.

Preheat an oven to 425° F.

Pour the oil into a medium-sized cast-iron or other heavy ovenproof skillet and place in the oven until sizzling hot, about 25 minutes.

If using fresh corn, cut the kernels from the cobs as described on page 11; there should be about 4 cups. Combine the corn, chile, flour, and salt and pepper to taste; mix well. Transfer the mixture to the hot oiled skillet, smoothing the top to form an even layer; do not stir. Gently press the corn mixture down to compact it. Bake until the corn mixture forms a bottom crust, about 30 minutes.

With a spatula, loosen the edges of the corn cake from the skillet. Invert a serving plate over the skillet and then invert the skillet. Remove skillet and serve corn cake hot. Cut into wedges at the table.

Serves 6.

VARIATION Omit the oil. Chop 6 slices of bacon. In the skillet that will be used for cooking the cake, cook the bacon over medium heat until crisp. Remove the bacon with a slotted spoon, reserving the drippings, and drain on paper toweling. Discard all but 3 tablespoons of the bacon drippings in the skillet. Heat the skillet in the oven as directed in the recipe. Stir the cooked bacon into the corn mixture. Bake as directed in the recipe.

¼ cup safflower or other high-quality vegetable oil
8 medium-sized ears fresh corn, or 4 cups drained canned or thawed frozen corn kernels
1 tablespoon minced fresh green or red hot chile, or to taste
⅓ cup all-purpose flour
Salt
Freshly ground black pepper

Smothered Cajun Corn
(*Maque Choux*)

12 ears fresh corn, or 6 cups drained canned or thawed frozen corn kernels
6 tablespoons (¾ stick) unsalted butter
1 cup finely chopped yellow onion
2 tablespoons granulated sugar
½ teaspoon salt, or to taste
Freshly ground black pepper
Ground cayenne or other dried hot chile
1½ cups peeled, seeded, and chopped ripe or drained canned tomatoes
1½ cups homemade chicken stock or canned chicken broth
½ cup heavy (whipping) cream or evaporated milk

It certainly wouldn't be traditional, but this venerable Cajun side dish also makes an excellent pasta sauce.

If using fresh corn, cut the kernels from the cobs as described on page 11; there should be about 6 cups. Reserve. If using canned or frozen corn, reserve.

In a sauté pan or heavy skillet, melt 2 tablespoons of the butter over medium-high heat. Add the onion and sauté until soft but not browned, about 5 minutes. Stir in the reserved corn, sugar, salt, and peppers to taste and sauté until the corn begins to stick to the pan, about 10 minutes. Stir in the tomatoes and sauté until liquid evaporates, about 5 minutes longer. Add the stock or broth and bring to a boil. Reduce the heat to low and cook, stirring frequently, until most of the liquid is absorbed, about 15 minutes longer.

Stir into the corn the remaining 4 tablespoons butter and the cream or evaporated milk. Cook, stirring frequently, until most of the liquid is absorbed, about 5 minutes.

Serves 6.

VARIATIONS For seafood *maque choux,* sauté 1 pound shrimp, peeled; shucked small oysters; or flaked crab or chopped lobster meat. Stir into the corn just before serving.

For poultry *maque choux,* brown about 1 pound boned, skinned chicken, duck, or pheasant, cut into bite-sized pieces, in the butter before adding the corn.

Corn and Wild Rice Sauté

6 medium-sized ears fresh corn,
preferably white, or 3 cups
drained canned or thawed
frozen corn kernels
2 tablespoons unsalted butter
2 tablespoons olive oil, preferably
extra-virgin
1 tablespoon minced or pressed garlic
2 cups cooked wild rice
3 tablespoons minced, well-drained
sun-dried tomatoes in olive oil
⅓ cup minced fresh basil
Salt
Freshly ground black pepper
Fresh basil sprigs for garnish
(optional)

Christy Hill, one of my favorite restaurants on the north shore of
Lake Tahoe, serves a side dish that is similar to this flavorful
concoction. The mixture also makes a great stuffing for fowl.

If using fresh corn, cut the kernels from the cobs as described on page 11;
there should be about 3 cups. Reserve. If using canned or frozen corn,
reserve.

In a sauté pan or skillet over medium-high heat, melt the butter with the
oil. Add the garlic and sauté about 30 seconds. Stir in the reserved corn,
wild rice, and tomatoes and sauté until the corn is cooked, about 4 minutes
for young corn, or up to 8 minutes for older corn. Stir in the minced basil
and salt and pepper to taste. Garnish with basil sprigs, if using. Serve
immediately.

Serves 6 as a side dish.

Corn-Season Pizza

For the cornmeal dough recipe, as well as detailed directions for making pizza, please refer to pages 17–25 in my book *Pizza*. Alternatively, use a favorite pizza crust recipe, substituting one part cornmeal to two parts flour for the flour measure, or purchase a ready-to-bake crust from a good take-out pizzeria.

Prepare the pizza dough and let rise as directed in recipe.

If possible, line the bottom of a gas oven or the bottom rack of an electric oven with unglazed quarry tiles. Alternatively, place a baking stone in the oven. Preheat oven to 500° F for about 1 hour before assembling the pizza.

If using fresh corn, cut the kernels from the cobs as described on page 11; there should be about 4 cups. Reserve. If using canned or frozen corn, reserve.

On a floured surface, roll out the dough into a 15- to 16-inch round, two 12-inch rounds, or four 8-inch rounds for individual pizzas.

Place a dough round on a cornmeal-dusted wooden pizza peel or well-oiled pizza screen or pizza pan with holes in bottom. Brush the dough all over with olive oil, then top with the mozzarella and smoked cheese, leaving a ½-inch border around the edges. Top the cheese with the reserved corn, then sprinkle with the garlic, onion, and salt and pepper to taste. Drizzle evenly with olive oil.

Transfer the pizza to the preheated baking surface and bake until the crust is golden and the cheese is bubbly, about 10 to 15 minutes. Remove from the oven to a cutting tray or board and lightly brush the edges of the crust with olive oil. Sprinkle the top with the Parmesan cheese and garnish with chives. Slice and serve immediately.

Serves 6 to 8 as an appetizer, or 4 as a main course.

Pizza dough (see recipe introduction)
8 medium-sized ears fresh corn,
    or 4 cups drained canned or
    thawed frozen corn kernels
Cornmeal for dusting pizza peel
    (paddle) or vegetable oil for
    brushing pizza screen or pan
About ½ cup olive oil, preferably
    extra-virgin
2½ cups (about 10 ounces) freshly
    shredded mozzarella cheese
1½ cups (about 6 ounces) freshly
    shredded smoked cheese such as
    Gouda or mozzarella
2 tablespoons minced or pressed
    garlic cloves, or to taste
½ cup chopped red onion
Salt
Freshly ground white pepper
½ cup (about 2 ounces) freshly grated
    Parmesan cheese
Whole or minced fresh chives for
    garnish

Corn Fritters

Serve as a savory side dish, plain or with dollops of sour cream and a favorite salsa. For a sweet breakfast treat or light dessert, sprinkle with powdered sugar or drizzle with warm maple syrup.

If using fresh corn, cut the kernels from the cobs as described on page 11; there should be about 2 cups. Reserve. If using canned or frozen corn, reserve.

In a medium-sized bowl, beat the egg yolks. Stir in the reserved corn, flour, butter, sugar, and salt, mixing thoroughly.

In a separate bowl, beat the egg whites until stiff but not dry. Fold them into the corn mixture.

Pour the oil into a deep-fat fryer or saucepan to a depth of about 2 inches. Place over high heat until temperature reaches 375° F, or until a small piece of bread dropped into the oil turns golden within seconds.

Using a heaping tablespoonful of batter for each fritter, drop the batter into the hot oil; do not crowd the pan. Cook, turning several times, until golden all over, about 6 to 7 minutes. With a slotted spoon, transfer fritters to paper toweling to drain. Cook remaining batter, adding oil to pan as needed. Serve warm.

Serves 6 to 8.

4 medium-sized ears fresh corn,
    or 2 cups drained canned or
    thawed frozen corn kernels
2 large eggs, separated
¼ cup all-purpose flour, preferably
    unbleached
2 tablespoons unsalted butter, melted
1½ teaspoons granulated sugar
¼ teaspoon salt, or to taste
About ¼ cup safflower or other
    high-quality vegetable oil, or as
    needed

Old-fashioned Corn Relish

10 ears fresh corn
2 tablespoons safflower or other
    high-quality vegetable oil
1 cup chopped white onion
1 cup diced red sweet pepper
2 tablespoons minced fresh green or
    red hot chile
⅔ cup dried currants
2 cups apple cider or distilled white
    vinegar
2 cups water
1 cup granulated sugar
1 teaspoon celery seeds
1 teaspoon mustard seeds
3 whole cloves
½ teaspoon Tabasco or other red
    pepper sauce, or to taste
½ teaspoon salt, or to taste
Boiling water for processing relish

Serve this tangy concoction with grilled or roasted meats or on burgers and other sandwiches.

Cut the kernels from the cobs as described on page 11; there should be about 5 cups.

Heat the oil in a large pot over medium-high heat. Add the corn and sauté for 2 minutes. Add the onion, sweet pepper, chile, currants, vinegar, water, sugar, celery and mustard seeds, cloves, pepper sauce, and salt. Bring to a boil, then reduce the heat to low and simmer, uncovered, for 35 minutes.

Spoon the relish into hot, sterilized jars, leaving about ¼ inch space at the top. Wipe the jar rims clean with paper toweling, cover with sterilized lids, and screw rings to close tightly. Transfer the jars to a canning kettle and pour in boiling water to cover jars by about 2 inches. Boil for 15 minutes. With canning tongs, transfer jars to counter-top to cool.

Store the jars in a cool, dark place for at least a week before using.

Makes 4 pints.

Corn-Studded Egg Bread

4 ears fresh yellow corn,
   or 2 cups drained canned or
   thawed frozen corn kernels
2 packages dry yeast
½ cup warm water (105° to 115° F)
1½ cups milk, warmed
¼ cup unsalted butter, melted and
   cooled slightly
½ cup granulated sugar
1 teaspoon salt
3 eggs
7½ cups all-purpose flour, preferably
   unbleached, or as needed
Cornmeal for dusting baking sheets
   or loaf pans
1 egg yolk mixed with 1 tablespoon
   milk for glaze
Black or white sesame seeds or poppy
   seeds for sprinkling on top

Until I tasted the moist version baked by my assistant Ellen Berger-Quan, I always thought of the Jewish egg bread called hallah (or challah) as a dry, boring loaf. Together we decided that corn would be an attractive, sweet alternative to the raisins that are usually scattered throughout the dough.

Cut the kernels from the cobs as described on page 11; there should be about 2 cups. Reserve. If using canned or frozen corn, reserve.

In a large bowl, sprinkle the yeast over the warm water and stir until dissolved. Add the milk, butter, sugar, salt, eggs, and reserved corn; mix well. Add 4 cups of the flour and blend well. Stir in the remaining 3½ cups flour. Turn the dough out onto a floured surface and knead until it is elastic and no longer sticky; add more flour, about 1 tablespoon at a time, if needed to achieve correct texture.

Shape the dough into a ball and place it in a large oiled bowl; turn ball to coat all surfaces. Cover and let rise in a warm place until doubled in bulk, about 1 hour.

Punch down the dough and let rise another 20 minutes. Generously grease 3 baking sheets or 9- by 5-inch loaf pans and dust lightly with cornmeal.

Divide the dough into 3 equal portions. Working with 1 portion at a time, divide the portion into thirds. Roll each third into a rope about 10 inches long. Braid the 3 ropes together, pinch ends together, and tuck ends under to seal. Push loaf from each end with hands to form a compact loaf. Place on prepared baking sheet or in pan. Braid the remaining 2 dough portions. Let loaves rise, uncovered, for 45 minutes.

Preheat an oven to 350° F.

Brush the tops of the bread loaves with the glaze and sprinkle with seeds. Bake until golden brown and a wooden skewer inserted in the center of each loaf comes out clean, about 20 to 35 minutes. Transfer bread to wire racks to cool. Serve warm or at room temperature.

Makes three 9-inch loaves.

Guatemalan Corn Beverage
(Atole)

I find this smooth, rich drink much more appealing than the Mexican and Southwest Indian drinks that are also called *atole*. The latter are made with cornmeal and water rather than the fresh kernels and milk used here.

Serve *atole* warm in mugs or heat-resistant glasses on a cold day. Or, for a refreshing summer treat, refrigerate and serve well chilled, without ice. Although delicious when offered plain, the drink, whether warm or cold, is traditionally topped with a bit of puréed, roasted and peeled red hot chile or red sweet pepper and a sprinkle of cooked corn kernels.

Cut the corn kernels from the cobs as described on page 11; there should be about 4 cups. Transfer to a food processor or blender and chop finely. Add about 1 cup of the milk and purée until smooth.

In a large, heavy saucepan over medium-high heat, combine the corn purée, the remaining 3 cups milk, the light cream or half-and-half, cinnamon sticks, vanilla bean, if using, sugar, and salt. Bring almost to a boil, then reduce the heat to low and simmer, uncovered, stirring frequently to keep the corn from sticking, until the mixture is reduced to the consistency of heavy cream, about 3 to 4 hours.

Remove and discard cinnamon sticks and vanilla bean from the corn mixture. If using vanilla extract, stir it in. Strain the mixture through a sieve lined with several layers of cheesecloth; squeeze the cheesecloth to release as much juice from the corn pulp as possible.

Pour warm strained liquid into mugs and serve immediately. Or cover and refrigerate until very cold and serve in chilled glasses.

Serves 6.

8 medium-sized ears fresh corn
4 cups milk
4 cups light cream or half-and-half
3 cinnamon sticks
1 vanilla bean, or 2 teaspoons vanilla extract
½ cup granulated sugar or unrefined Mexican sugar (*piloncillo*), or to taste
¼ teaspoon salt, or to taste

Corn Ice Cream

4 medium-sized ears fresh corn
3 cups heavy (whipping) cream
1½ cups milk
Peel from 2 lemons, removed in long
    strips
½ vanilla bean, or 2 teaspoons vanilla
    extract
¼ teaspoon salt
10 egg yolks
1⅓ cups granulated sugar

It may sound bizarre, but milky fresh corn makes an ice cream with sensationally rich flavor and a very smooth texture. Use the sweetest-tasting and creamiest corn available.

Cut the corn kernels from the cobs as described on page 11; there should be about 2 cups.

In a saucepan over medium heat, combine the corn and ¼ cup of the cream and cook until the corn is tender, about 5 minutes. Transfer to a food processor or blender and purée until smooth. Reserve.

In a saucepan over medium-high heat, combine 1½ cups of the cream, the milk, lemon peel, vanilla bean (if using), and salt. Bring to a boil, then remove from the heat and reserve.

Meanwhile, combine the egg yolks, sugar, and reserved corn purée in a heavy saucepan. Slowly whisk or beat in the remaining 1¼ cups cream. Cook over medium-low heat, stirring constantly, until the mixture coats the back of a spoon, about 12 minutes; do not boil. Remove from the heat and stir in the reserved warm cream mixture; remove and discard the lemon peel and vanilla bean, if used. Add the vanilla extract, if using. Pour the mixture into a bowl and let cool to room temperature. Cover tightly and refrigerate until cold, at least several hours or as long as overnight.

Strain the chilled corn mixture through a wire sieve into an ice cream maker and freeze according to manufacturer's instructions.

Makes about 1½ quarts; serves 6 to 8.

DRIED

Most of the corn grown for human consumption is in the form of dried corn or derivative products, ranging from popcorn kernels still attached to the cob to highly refined pulverized cornstarch. Many of our favorite foods are made from dried corn, the majority from dent or field corn (page 6).

I could easily fill a book with recipes for Italian polenta-based dishes, another with American cornbreads, and a third volume with Mexican corn specialties. In the limited space of this book, I've put together a very subjective collection of personal favorites that I hope will become staples in your kitchen.

For crunchy texture and exciting flavor, cornmeal can be added to almost any regular bread dough, but usually no more than as a substitution for one-half cup of the specified flour. Since so little cornmeal is used in such bread recipes, I have not included any of them here. Instead I have concentrated on variations for quick cornbread, where corn plays the starring role.

DRIED CORN RECIPES IN OTHER JAMES McNAIR COOKBOOKS:

CHEESE COOKBOOK:

Bacon and Cheese Spoon Bread, page 64

Cheese Grits Soufflé, page 63

Stacked Cheese Enchiladas with Mole Sauce, page 67

CHICKEN:

Chicken Enchiladas with Green Chili Sauce, page 63

Chicken and Spinach Pie in Polenta Pastry, page 68

Chicken Tamale Pie, page 72

COLD CUISINE:

Summer Berry and Polenta Pudding, page 81

GRILL COOKBOOK:

Herbed Polenta, page 69

ALL-AMERICAN POPCORN

Well over 400 million pounds of popcorn kernels are exploded in the United States each year. This popular American food has come a long way since it was introduced to the Plymouth colonists by their native guests at the first Thanksgiving feast.

The Indians tossed the kernels directly onto hot stones heated in a campfire. Today, however, a wide variety of automatic popcorn machines or a microwave oven can be used. To make popcorn without oil, purchase unflavored popcorn packaged for microwave ovens or invest in a hot-air electric popper; follow manufacturer's directions. A cup of unadorned popped corn contains only about 25 calories.

When using a popper that requires fat for popping, place 2 tablespoons vegetable oil and 1 or 2 popcorn kernels in the popper. Heat until the temperature reaches about 420° F and the kernels explode, then stir in ½ cup kernels. For stove-top popping without a special popper, select a large, heavy pot with a lid that allows steam to escape. Place the pot over high heat and preheat 2 tablespoons oil and a couple of popcorn kernels. When the kernels pop, add about 1 cup popcorn, or no more than a single layer of kernels in bottom of the pan. Shake the pan to keep kernels moving. Remove from heat when popping slows to about 3 seconds between pops.

The Dried-Corn Pantry

Corn flour. Cornmeal ground and sifted until it is very fine. Widely used by commercial bakers. Sometimes sold in retail markets as fish-fry coating.

Cornmeal. White, yellow, blue, and occasionally red corn kernels ground to varying degrees, from fine to coarse. Today most commercial cornmeal is milled with steel rollers that filter out the fibrous husk and the oil-rich germ, creating a drier meal with longer shelf life. More flavorful, old-fashioned stone-ground (sometimes called water-ground) cornmeal is crushed by water-driven millstones and includes the complete kernel—hull, starch, and germ. For optimum freshness, grind small batches of dried corn at home with a stone-wheel mill.

Cornstarch. Mainly used to thicken liquids, this product is pulverized from highly refined starch. Called corn flour in Britain.

Dried corn husks (*hojas de maiz*). Removed from large ears of field corn. Used for wrapping tamales. Available from Mexican groceries and some supermarkets.

Flint corn. Most often sold as Indian corn for decorative purposes, although it is edible when ground. Includes popular blue and rarer red corn from the Southwest.

Grits. Finely ground dried hominy.

Hominy. Whole kernels of dried dent or flint corn that have been treated in slaked-lime water to remove tough outer hulls. Sometimes called samp. In the Southwest hominy is known as *posole,* and in Mexico as *nixtamal.* May be purchased dried (dehydrated), frozen, or canned in water, its most widely available form.

Mexican corn dough (*masa*). Ground from partially cooked hulled corn (hominy or *nixtamal*). Make your own (page 53), purchase from a tortilla factory or Mexicatessen, or substitute Mexican corn flour (*masa harina*).

Mexican corn flour *(masa harina)*. Finely ground dehydrated *masa* dough. Check the ethnic-foods section of supermarkets or Mexican groceries.

Polenta. Refers both to a coarse grind of cornmeal from Italy and a mush made from cornmeal. Substitute any coarse cornmeal for a grainy texture, or finer cornmeal for a smoother consistency.

Popcorn. Sold on the cob or loose in white, yellow, black, blue, red, and multicolored; all pop up white.

STORING

To store dried corn, place whole ears in a large glass or plastic container with a tight-fitting lid, or enclose in large, sealable plastic bags. Store loose dried kernels in a tightly sealed jar or plastic bag. Keep in a cool place or in the refrigerator.

Recent hybridization of extremely high-yielding corn has produced a grain that goes rancid quickly after milling, especially the stone-ground meal that includes the oily corn germ. Some purists choose to grind dried corn at home and keep it refrigerated for no longer than five days. Small amounts of corn can be ground in a hand grinder or even in a blender. For larger amounts or for frequent grinding, choose a heavy-duty electric mill, preferably with a stone grinder.

In lieu of grinding at home, purchase commercially ground meal and other dried corn in small quantities and use as soon as possible. Place in sealed jars or plastic bags in a cool spot or in the refrigerator. Although some vitamin content will be lost in the cold environment, stone-ground cornmeal will keep refrigerated for up to three months or frozen for up to six months; regular steel-ground meal will keep for longer periods.

Always check dried corn for pest infestation and smell for rancidity before cooking. Fresh dried corn products should smell sweet.

To reheat cold popcorn, spread it in a shallow roasting pan and place in a preheated 250° F oven. Heat, stirring occasionally, until warm, about 20 to 25 minutes.

Although some of us prefer it plain, Americans have developed a love affair with flavored popcorn, with entire stores devoted to the stuff. For home-fresh flavor, pour 6 to 8 cups hot popped corn into a large bowl, sprinkle with salt to taste, and drizzle with about ¼ cup melted butter or half melted butter and half olive oil. Stir to coat well, then toss in one of the following:

About 3 tablespoons minced mixed fresh herbs such as oregano, rosemary, sage, or thyme, or 1 tablespoon crumbled dried herbs, one kind or a mixture

About 2 teaspoons ground dried hot chile mixed with 1 teaspoon ground cumin

⅔ cup crumbled blue or goat's milk cheese or freshly shredded Cheddar, Parmesan, jalapeño Jack, or other cheese.

For garlic popcorn, simmer about 1 teaspoon minced or pressed garlic in the butter before drizzling it over the popcorn.

Hulled Dried Corn or Hominy (*Nixtamal*)

This ancient method of removing hard hulls from dried corn produces half-cooked whole kernels known as hominy in most of North America, *posole* in the Southwest, and *nixtamal* in Mexico. The corn is then ground to make *masa*, the dough used for making tortillas and tamales. While most of us will opt to buy canned hominy or dried *posole* and make tortillas or tamales out of Mexican corn flour *(masa harina)*, all of these dishes will be even tastier when prepared with homemade hominy.

In a heavy enameled, stainless steel, or other nonreactive pan, combine the lime and water. Place over high heat and stir until the lime dissolves and the mixture comes to a boil. Add the corn and stir well. Remove any kernels that float to the top. Return to a boil and simmer for about 20 minutes for tortilla dough, or about 25 minutes for hominy, *posole,* or tamale dough. Remove from heat, cover, and let stand for about 1 hour for hominy, *posole,* or tamale dough, or at least several hours or as long as overnight for tortilla dough.

Drain the corn in a colander and rub the kernels between fingertips to remove remnants of the hulls. Rinse in cold water until the water is clear and all traces of debris are removed.

For hominy or *posole,* pull off the pointed germ end of each kernel, if you wish corn to splay into blossomlike puffs. Simmer kernels until tender and use as directed in recipes, cover and refrigerate for up to 1 week, or freeze in freezer bags for up to 6 months.

To make tortilla or tamale dough, dry the rinsed hulled corn with paper toweling. Put the corn through a stone-wheel grinder until it resembles grits. Mix in just enough water, about ⅔ to ¾ cup, to make a stiff dough that holds together. Use as directed in recipes, or cover and refrigerate for up to 3 days, or freeze in freezer containers or bags for up to 6 months.

Makes about 8 cups hominy or *posole*, or 2 to 2½ pounds tortilla or tamale dough.

2 tablespoons powdered slaked lime or builder's lime (calcium hydroxide), available from builder's supply stores
2 quarts water
4 cups dried dent (field) or flint (Indian) corn (about 1½ pounds kernels), available from natural-foods stores or miller's supply catalogs, rinsed well to remove chaff

Southwestern Stewed Dried Corn (*Posole*)

1 package (1 pound) dried white or
   blue hominy (*posole*), 2 cans
   (16 ounces *each*) white or yellow
   hominy, drained and rinsed, or
   Hulled Dried Corn or Hominy
   (page 53)
1 cup chopped yellow onion
1 tablespoon minced or pressed garlic
2 pounds boneless pork loin, cut into
   small bite-sized pieces
1 pound boneless beef sirloin, top
   loin, or other tender cut, cut
   into small bite-sized pieces
4 whole dried New Mexico chiles,
   stems and seeds removed, or
   2 tablespoons ground dried hot
   chile, or to taste
4 green onions, including green tops,
   chopped
1 tablespoon salt, or to taste
Freshly ground black pepper

CONDIMENTS

Minced fresh oregano or dried
   oregano
Chopped red, white, or green onion
Minced garlic
Minced fresh or canned hot or mild
   green chiles
Chopped ripe tomato

In Santa Fe, Socoro Sandoval showed me her slow-simmering way of making this Southwest staple. As in so many other Spanish homes, no Christmas, New Year, wedding, fiesta, homecoming, or other important event at the Sandovals is complete without this comforting dish. Although *posole* is delicious on its own, fiery Red Chile Sauce (page 92) spooned over the top makes it even better.

Socoro starts with dehydrated *posole,* but many other cooks with limited time use canned hominy.

Rinse the dried *posole* and discard any blemished pieces. Place dried *posole* or drained hominy in a stockpot and add the yellow onion, garlic, and water to cover. Bring to a boil over high heat. Reduce the heat to low, cover the pot, and simmer until the corn is soft and puffed, about 45 minutes for canned hominy, or up to 3 hours for dried *posole;* add a little water as needed to the dried *posole* to keep it covered.

Add the pork, beef, chiles or ground chile, green onions, and salt and pepper to taste. Simmer until the meat is very tender, at least 2 hours or as long as 6 hours. Skim occasionally and add water as needed if the *posole* gets too dry.

To ready the condiments, place the oregano, onion, garlic, chiles, and tomato in separate small bowls, for adding at the table. Ladle the stew into soup bowls and serve piping hot.

Serves 6.

Tortillas

½ recipe tortilla dough (page 53)
or 2 cups Mexican corn flour
(masa harina)
About 1⅓ cups warm water,
if using corn flour

The best-tasting tortillas start with dough made from *nixtamal* (page 53). For convenience, Mexican corn flour *(masa harina)* can be substituted.

Prepare the tortilla dough as directed. If using corn flour, combine it in a bowl with just enough of the warm water to form a dough that holds together.

Divide the dough into 12 equal-sized pieces and roll each piece between your palms to form a smooth ball. As each ball is formed, transfer it to a bowl and cover bowl with a damp cloth or moist paper toweling until all the balls are formed.

Place a ball of dough between 2 sheets of waxed paper. Flatten the dough with your hand, then roll out with a rolling pin, turning the waxed paper over several times and rolling in all directions to form a round about 9 inches in diameter. Peel off the waxed paper. If desired, trim the dough into a perfect round with a small, sharp knife, using a saucer as a guide.

Alternatively, put each dough ball between two sheets of waxed paper and place it in a tortilla press, positioning the ball slightly toward the back of the center of the press. Close press tightly. Open press and remove tortilla; peel away waxed paper.

To cook tortillas, heat a griddle or large, heavy skillet over medium-high heat. Add tortilla and cook until the bottom is lightly speckled with brown, about 30 seconds. Flip over with a wide spatula and cook until the other side is done, about 1 minute longer. Wrap in aluminum foil to keep warm while cooking remaining tortillas. Serve immediately or cool, wrap tightly, and refrigerate up to 1 week.

To reheat, wrap tortillas tightly in foil and place in a preheated 350° F oven for 15 minutes. Alternatively, enclose tortillas in plastic wrap and place in a microwave oven set at high for about 6 seconds per tortilla.

Makes 12 tortillas.

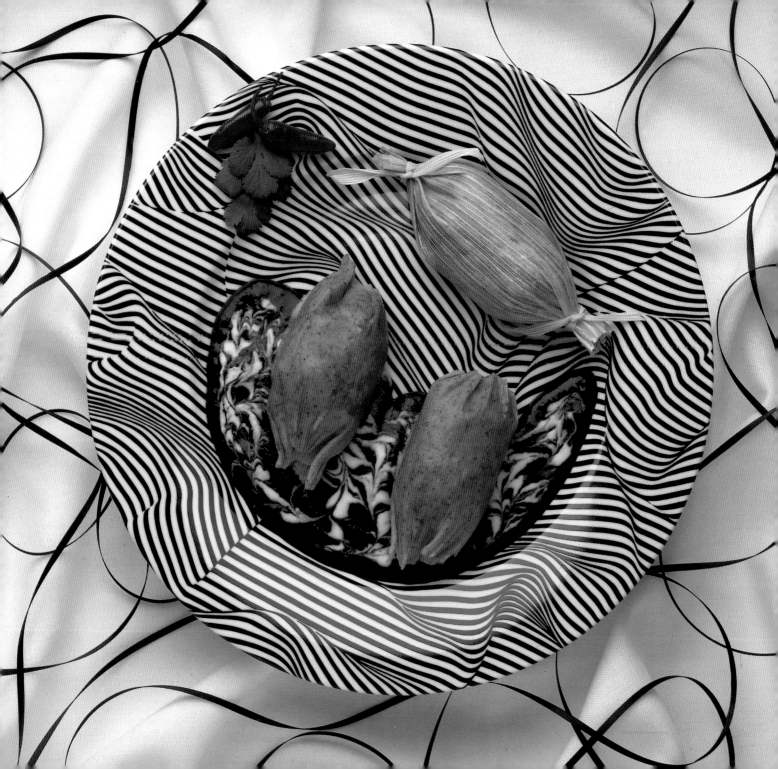

Chicken Tamales with
Black and White Bean Sauces

I've chosen a simple chicken filling to illustrate how to make tamales. They could instead be stuffed with cooked duck, pheasant, turkey, or other fowl. Use this basic recipe to create an infinite variety of tamales; try the filling suggestions on the next two pages or create your own tamale stuffings from complementary mixtures.

If you're lucky enough to live near a Mexican grocery or tortilla factory (tortilleria) that sells fresh masa (ground partially cooked hulled corn), by all means use it in the dough in place of the more readily available corn flour. Or, grind your own masa from freshly hulled hominy (page 53).

Tamales may also be wrapped in banana leaves for an exotic appearance or in aluminum foil for a less-glamorous presentation. No matter how you wrap them, serve the tamales piping hot with the suggested bean sauces, or with Red Chile Sauce (page 92), a favorite salsa, or a mole or tomato sauce.

Place the corn husks in a large bowl and cover with warm water. Soak to soften, at least 1 hour or as long as overnight.

Prepare the bean sauces as directed; reserve.

To prepare the dough, place the lard, butter, or shortening in a bowl and beat until light and fluffy. Stir in the freshly ground hominy or corn flour, baking powder, and chile. If using fresh dough, add ⅓ cup of the stock or diluted broth; if using corn flour, add ¾ cup of the liquid. With your hands, mix the dough until it clings together in a ball, adding more liquid if needed. Season to taste with salt. Let stand at room temperature for at least 15 minutes, or cover and refrigerate for up to 3 days; bring to room temperature before using.

1 package (8 ounces) dried corn husks (*hojas de maiz*)
2 cups Black Bean Sauce (page 93)
1 cup White Bean Sauce (page 93)

TAMALE DOUGH
⅔ cup high-quality pork lard (in Spanish, *manteca*; available in Mexican markets), unsalted butter, or solid vegetable shortening, at room temperature
½ recipe freshly ground hominy for tamale dough (page 53; do not mix with water), or 2 cups Mexican corn flour (*masa harina*)
1 teaspoon baking powder
2 tablespoons ground dried hot chile, preferably *ancho* or *pasilla* chile, or puréed roasted, seeded, and deveined fresh hot chile
About 1 cup lukewarm homemade light chicken stock, or ½ cup canned chicken broth mixed with ½ cup water
Salt

→

CHICKEN FILLING

1 tablespoon vegetable oil
¾ cup finely chopped onion
1 teaspoon minced or pressed garlic
2 cups cooked chopped or shredded
    chicken
¼ cup Red Chile Sauce (page 92) or
    canned red chile sauce (available
    in Mexican markets or ethnic
    section of some supermarkets)
3 tablespoons chopped fresh cilantro
    (coriander)
Salt
Small whole red chiles for garnish
Fresh cilantro leaflets for garnish

To prepare the filling, heat the oil in a sauté pan or skillet over medium-high heat. Add the onion and sauté until golden, about 10 minutes. Add the garlic and sauté about 1 minute longer. Stir in the chicken, chile sauce, and chopped cilantro. Cook about 2 minutes. Season to taste with salt; reserve.

To assemble tamales, shake excess water off the soaked corn husks and pat husks dry with paper toweling. Lay 1 large husk or overlap 2 medium-sized husks on a flat surface, smooth side up. Form a rectangle in the center of the husk with about 3 tablespoons of the dough, leaving about 2 inches uncovered husk at each end and about ½ inch on either side. Spoon about 2 tablespoons of the filling down the center of the dough. Fold the husk sides up and overlap loosely to allow for expansion during cooking. Tie each end with narrow strips of torn husk, cotton string, or nonsoluble ribbon or twine. For a festive presentation, use scissors to fringe the ends of the wrappers. Alternatively, the husks may be overlapped and tied to form square or rectangular packages as described on page 24.

Line a steamer rack with extra husks. Stack the tamales, seam side down, on the rack in up to 3 layers. Position rack over several inches of simmering water. Place a cloth kitchen towel over top layer to keep excess water from dripping over tamales. Cover with a tight-fitting lid or aluminum foil. Steam over medium-low heat or in a preheated 450° oven until the tamale dough is plump, slightly firm, and easily comes free from the wrapper, about 45 to 55 minutes; unwrap a tamale to test for doneness.

Reheat the bean sauces. Spoon some of the Black Bean Sauce onto each dinner plate. Drizzle the White Bean Sauce over the black sauce, then pull a wooden skewer through the sauces to create an attractive pattern. Unwrap tamales and arrange on top of the sauces. Garnish with whole chiles and cilantro leaflets.

Makes about 16 tamales; serves 6 to 8.

TAMALE VARIATIONS

Prepare the tamale dough as described on the preceding pages. Substitute any of the following or your own favorite fillings for the chicken filling. Complete the tamales as described in the basic recipe or as specified.

Black Bean Tamales. Sauté ¾ cup chopped yellow onion in 2 tablespoons vegetable oil, stir in 1 teaspoon minced or pressed garlic, 2 cups well-drained, cooked black beans, ¼ cup chopped fresh cilantro (coriander), and ground dried hot chile, ground cumin, and salt to taste.

Cheese Tamales. Fill with about 12 ounces freshly shredded Cheddar or Monterey Jack cheese or crumbled goat's milk or blue cheese.

Corn-Filled Tamales. Fill with about 2 cups Sautéed Fresh Corn (page 14).

Grilled Fish Tamales. Using about 1 pound fish, brush ½-inch-thick fillets of salmon, sturgeon, swordfish, or other firm-fleshed fish with melted butter and grill over a hot fire just until well seared on the outside. Cut pieces to fit within the rectangle of tamale dough.

Meat Tamales. Fill with sliced grilled beef or pork blended with Red Chile Sauce. Alternatively, prepare about 2 cups of a favorite recipe for any spicy meat filling, or use my recipe for Chili con Carne (page 76, *James McNair's Beef Cookbook*).

Mushroom Tamales. Chop 1 pound fresh mushrooms, preferably wild varieties, and sauté in 3 tablespoons butter or olive oil. Season with salt, freshly ground black pepper, and minced fresh sage or thyme.

Shellfish Tamales. Grill or sauté about 1 pound shrimp, peeled; lobster tail meat; or scallops. Coarsely chop and combine with green chile sauce or green salsa. Serve with the same sauce used in the filling.

SWEET TAMALES

Serve sweet tamales as a snack, dessert, or side dish. Prepare the tamale dough as directed on page 61, adding ½ to ¾ cup granulated sugar along with the ground hominy or corn flour; adjust amount of sugar according to sweetness of the selected filling. Most Mexican tamale makers use lard and stock or broth in sweet tamale dough. You may find that using butter for the fat and milk for the liquid more compatible with your taste. Omit the ground chile, if you wish, although it adds an interesting counterpoint to the sweet filling.

Fill with about 2 cups of one of the following:
Mincemeat
Mashed cooked pumpkin or other
    squash
Creamed Fresh Corn (page 14)
Raisins
Chopped banana or tropical fruits

Alternatively, stir about ¾ cup of one of the following into the dough and omit filling:
Chopped toasted nuts
Grated fresh coconut
Chopped dried fruit
Puréed berries

Basic Polenta

Cornmeal mush, porridge, or gruel certainly tastes much better than these English names make it sound. This comforting food is infinitely more appealing when called by its colonial American moniker, hasty pudding, or by one of its European titles, especially Italian polenta, the term now commonly used in the United States. On both sides of the Atlantic the dish is enjoyed two ways: *soft,* with the texture of cream of wheat, served in a bowl and eaten with a spoon; or *firm,* cooked until stiff and then sliced and eaten warm, or chilled and then sliced and reheated until a crisp crust forms.

Indians of the American Southwest turn blue cornmeal into *atole,* a beverage, or into *chauquehue,* a gray mush that is sometimes flavored with honey and served as a cure for stomachaches. New Englanders and Canadians are likely to prepare a breakfast mush made from yellow cornmeal and dress it with melted butter and maple syrup or brown sugar. Southerners enjoy grits, a mush made from ground hominy, topped with melted butter and salt and perhaps fried eggs or gravy. When I was a youngster in Louisiana, I would eat grits only if they were served with butter and white sugar. In the southern part of my home state, Cajuns cook up their *couche-couche* (yellow cornmeal mush) and drizzle it with milk and dark cane syrup. Since colonial times Americans everywhere have enjoyed sliced leftover mush panfried in butter or other fat.

Italians ladle soft mush, or *polentina,* into bowls and adorn it with creamy Gorgonzola or mascarpone cheese and/or shower it with freshly grated Parmesan. It may also be offered as a first course with a variety of sauces, in the same manner as pasta. *Polentina* is sometimes served with warm milk as a nourishing dish for children or ailing adults; a sprinkle of sugar turns the dish into a dessert or snack.

Polenta is the Italian name for both the cornmeal and the cooked mush. The finished dish may be served freshly cooked as a side dish or as a bed for cooked meats. Frequently it is cooled, then sliced or

→

2 cups cornmeal (see recipe
   introduction)
1 tablespoon salt, or to taste
10 cups cold water, homemade stock,
   or canned broth for soft mush
   (*polentina*), or 6 cups cold
   water, homemade stock, or
   canned broth for firm mush
   (polenta)

TOPPINGS FOR SOFT MUSH OR POLENTINA

Sour cream or plain yogurt
Mascarpone, Gorgonzola, or other
   soft creamy cheese
Freshly grated Parmesan cheese
Fresh tomato sauce, Italian meat
   sauce, mushroom sauce, or
   other favorite pasta sauce
Melted butter or olive oil
Maple syrup, brown sugar, or honey

OPTIONAL ADDITIONS TO FIRM POLENTA

½ cup (1 stick) unsalted butter
⅔ cup freshly grated Parmesan cheese
2 cups shredded good-melting cheese
   such as fontina or crumbled
   goat's milk cheese
2 tablespoons minced fresh herb of
   choice, or 2 teaspoons crumbled
   dried herb of choice
1 cup sautéed fresh wild mushrooms
   such as chanterelles or porcini
1 cup chopped cooked spinach, Swiss
   chard, or other greens

Butter or olive oil for reheating firm
   polenta

cut into fanciful shapes and reheated for a side dish or used as a component in other dishes. Leftover polenta is handled in the same way.

Although in the United States we identify Italian mush with the coarse yellow cornmeal sold here as polenta, in Italy the type of cornmeal cooked into *polentina* or polenta varies with the region. Finely ground yellow or white cornmeal is favored in the Veneto; a coarse yellow meal is preferred in Piedmont and Lombardy. Successful polenta can be made with stone-ground, water-ground, or regular American cornmeal in yellow, white, and even blue or red.

In Romania, freshly cooked cornmeal, or *mamaliga,* is crowned with tangy sour cream or yogurt. The French prepare *millas,* adding a bit of lard to the cooking liquid, or *armotte,* stirring in pieces of crisp goose or pork after the cornmeal is cooked. Both dishes can be served warm or they can be cooled until set, cut into slices, and grilled or panfried.

For Caribbean mush, or *coo-coo,* sliced okra is simmered along with the cornmeal, or the cornmeal is cooked in coconut milk instead of water.

Preparing polenta in a microwave oven does not save much cooking time, but it does save a lot of stirring time. Plus, it produces virtually foolproof results. Directions follow the stovetop method. In either case, stirring the cornmeal into cold water before heating prevents lumps from forming during cooking.

In a heavy saucepan or copper polenta pan, combine the cornmeal, salt, and water, stock, or broth; stir well. Place over medium-high heat and bring to a simmer, stirring occasionally with a wooden spoon. Reduce the heat to low and simmer, stirring frequently and scraping the bottom of the pot with the spoon, until done to the soft or firm state described below.

For soft mush *(polentina),* cook until the mixture thickens to the texture of cream of wheat, about 25 to 30 minutes; add more liquid if necessary to achieve a smooth, soft consistency. Pour into large, shallow individual bowls, add one or more of the suggested toppings, and serve steaming hot.

Or, transfer to the top portion of a double boiler set over simmering water and keep warm; stir in more of the same cooking liquid as needed to keep the mixture pourable until serving time.

For firm mush (polenta), cook until the mixture comes away from the sides of the pan and is thick enough to hold the wooden spoon upright, about 35 to 45 minutes total cooking time. Remove from the heat and, if desired, stir in any one or a compatible combination of the suggested additions. Stir until the butter or cheese melts, if using. Pour the mixture onto a platter or other flat surface and smooth the top with a damp wooden spoon. Alternatively, pour the polenta into a bowl that has been dampened with water, then unmold onto a serving plate. Cut warm polenta into wedges and serve warm.

For polenta that is to be reheated later or used in other dishes, cook as directed for firm polenta, stir in any selected additions as directed, then pour the mixture into a generously buttered 9- by 5-inch loaf pan. Cool to room temperature, then cover and refrigerate for at least 2 hours or as long as 3 days. Turn the chilled loaf out onto a cutting surface and slice or cut into fanciful shapes. Use as directed in recipes or panfry in butter or olive oil. You can also brush the slices with butter or olive oil and heat them on a charcoal grill, under a broiler, or in a toaster until crispy on the outside and heated through.

MICROWAVE POLENTA Combine the cornmeal, salt, and liquid in a 2-quart glass dish and cook on high for 6 minutes in a regular-sized microwave oven, or for 9 minutes in a small oven. Stir, then cover loosely with paper toweling and continue cooking for 6 minutes longer in a regular-sized oven, or for 9 minutes longer in a small microwave. Remove from the oven. For soft mush (polentina), pour into bowls and serve with selected toppings. For firm mush (polenta), stir in selected additions, let stand for 3 minutes, then pour onto a platter and serve warm, or pour into a buttered loaf pan and chill.

Serves 6 to 8 as a side dish.

POLENTA PIE

Prepare firm Basic Polenta, chill, and cut into 3-inch squares. Arrange a layer of the squares in the bottom of a buttered 9- by 13-inch baking dish.

Preheat an oven to 350° F.

Slice 1 pound fresh porcini or other wild mushroom varieties and sauté until soft with 4 ounces pancetta (Italian-style bacon), diced, in 3 tablespoons olive oil. Layer sautéed mushroom mixture over polenta squares and sprinkle with about 3 tablespoons minced fresh sage. Top with another layer of polenta squares, cover with about 2 cups shredded mozzarella or other good-melting cheese, and sprinkle with about ½ cup freshly grated Parmesan cheese.

Bake until the cheese is bubbly, about 30 minutes. Cool slightly, then cut into wedges or squares.

Serves 6.

VARIATION Prepare the polenta pie as described, substituting any favorite lasagna filling for the mushroom mixture.

Fried Polenta with Red Chile Sauce and Chorizo-Corn Sauté

Serve this zesty combo as a one-dish brunch or supper.

Prepare the firm polenta as described for reheating; chill.

Prepare the chile sauce; reserve.

In a bowl, combine the crème fraîche or sour cream, lime juice, and chopped mint and stir to mix thoroughly; reserve.

In a sauté pan or skillet, heat the 2 tablespoons oil over medium-low heat. Add the chorizo and cook, stirring occasionally to break up the meat, until done, about 10 minutes. With a slotted spoon, transfer to a small bowl. Discard all but 2 tablespoons fat from the skillet. Add the corn and sauté until the corn is tender, about 4 minutes for young corn, or 8 minutes for older corn. Stir in the reserved chorizo. Keep warm or reheat just before serving.

Turn the polenta out onto a cutting surface. Cut into ½-inch-thick slices and trim slices into squares or cut on the diagonal into triangles. Heat the ¼ cup butter or oil in a sauté pan or skillet over medium-high heat. Add the polenta and cook, turning once, until lightly browned and crisp on both sides.

To serve, reheat the chile sauce to serving temperature. Spoon the warm sauce into individual shallow bowls or onto plates. Arrange 2 or 3 polenta slices in the center of each pool of sauce and spoon the chorizo-corn mixture around the edge of the plate or over the top of the polenta. Drizzle with the reserved minted cream, garnish with lime zest or mint sprigs, and serve immediately.

Serves 6.

Basic Polenta (page 65)
Red Chile Sauce (page 92)
1 cup crème fraîche or sour cream
2 tablespoons freshly squeezed lime juice
3 tablespoons finely chopped fresh mint
2 tablespoons olive oil
¾ pound chorizo (Spanish-style pork sausage), crumbled
2 cups fresh, canned, or thawed frozen corn kernels
About ¼ cup (½ stick) unsalted butter or olive oil for sautéing
Lime zest or fresh mint sprigs for garnish

Three-Corn Tart

Mary King, an accomplished San Francisco cook, shared this recipe. It uses a trio of corn forms—cornmeal, corn flour, and whole kernels.

Melt the butter in a small pan. Add the garlic and chile and sauté until the garlic is soft but not browned, about 30 seconds; reserve.

In a saucepan, combine the cornmeal and chicken stock or broth; stir well. Place over medium-high heat and bring to a simmer, stirring occasionally with a wooden spoon. Reduce the heat to low and simmer, stirring frequently and scraping the bottom of the pan with the spoon, until the cornmeal is thick and smooth, about 15 minutes. Stir in the reserved seasoned butter. Pour the mixture into a 10-inch tart pan with a removable bottom, spreading evenly to the edges. Cover and chill until firm, about 1 hour.

Preheat an oven to 350° F.

Heat the oil in a sauté pan or skillet over medium-high heat. Add the chicken or turkey and sauté until the meat loses its pinkness, about 3 minutes. Add the chile sauce and continue cooking until most of the liquid evaporates, about 5 minutes longer. Stir in 2 tablespoons of the corn flour. Spread mixture evenly over the chilled crust. Grate the frozen cheese and sprinkle over the chicken or turkey mixture.

Combine the tomatoes and corn in a food processor or blender and coarsely purée. Stir in the remaining tablespoon of corn flour. Spread puréed mixture over the cheese layer. Bake for 25 minutes. Sprinkle with the Jack cheese and return to the oven until the cheese melts, about 5 minutes. Remove from the oven and let cool about 10 minutes. Remove from the tart ring and garnish with sweet pepper, cilantro, and nasturtium, if using. Serve warm.

Serves 6 as a first course, or 2 to 4 as a main course.

VARIATION For a red version, substitute ¼ pound chorizo sausage, crumbled, for the turkey or chicken. Use red chile sauce in place of green chile sauce, red tomatoes in place of yellow tomatoes, and red sweet peppers in place of golden peppers.

2 tablespoons unsalted butter
1 teaspoon minced or pressed garlic
2 teaspoons ground dried hot chile
⅔ cup coarsely ground cornmeal
2½ cups homemade chicken stock or canned chicken broth
1 teaspoon vegetable oil
¼ pound ground chicken or turkey
2 tablespoons homemade or canned green chile sauce
3 tablespoons Mexican corn flour (*masa harina*)
6 ounces cream cheese, frozen
¼ pound yellow tomatoes
1 cup cooked fresh, drained canned, or thawed frozen yellow corn kernels
4 ounces Monterey Jack cheese with hot chiles, freshly shredded
Roasted golden sweet peppers, cut into julienne for garnish
Fresh cilantro (coriander) sprigs for garnish
Pesticide-free nasturtiums for garnish (optional)

Golden Hominy and Corn Stew with Cornmeal Dumplings

1 cup dried baby lima or French *flageolet* beans
¼ cup olive oil
2 cups chopped yellow onion
1 tablespoon minced or pressed garlic
4 or 5 whole cloves
2 bay leaves
2 tablespoons minced fresh thyme, or 2 teaspoons crumbled dried thyme
2 quarts homemade vegetable or chicken stock or canned chicken broth
1 can (16 ounces) golden hominy, drained
1 cup diced carrot
1 cup diced, peeled turnip or rutabaga
½ cup minced fresh parsley
1 cup peeled, seeded, and chopped ripe or drained canned tomato
2 cups fresh, drained canned, or thawed frozen yellow corn
Salt
Freshly ground black pepper
Ground cayenne pepper

CORN DUMPLINGS
½ cup yellow cornmeal
½ cup cake flour
2 teaspoons baking powder
½ teaspoon salt
1 teaspoon granulated sugar
1 egg, lightly beaten
⅓ cup milk
1 tablespoon unsalted butter, melted
½ cup cooked fresh, drained canned, or thawed frozen yellow corn

A quartet of corn stars in this flavorful stew: Yellow hominy and fresh kernels are cooked with a host of other vegetables, then the dish is crowned with dumplings made of yellow cornmeal and more whole kernels.

To prepare the stew, carefully pick over the beans to remove any shriveled beans and foreign matter. Place in a bowl, cover with water, and soak overnight. Drain and reserve.

Heat the oil in a stockpot over medium-high heat. Add the onion and sauté until soft but not browned, about 5 minutes. Add the garlic and sauté 1 minute longer. Add the drained beans, cloves, bay leaves, thyme, and stock or broth. Bring to a boil, then reduce the heat to low and simmer, uncovered, for 45 minutes.

Add the drained hominy, carrot, turnip or rutabaga, parsley, and tomato and simmer until the vegetables are almost tender, about 30 minutes longer.

While the stew is simmering, prepare the dumpling batter. In a bowl, combine the cornmeal, flour, baking powder, salt, and sugar; mix well. Add the egg, milk, butter, and corn and stir until blended. Let stand about 10 minutes for cornmeal to absorb liquids before cooking.

Stir the corn into the stew and season to taste with salt and peppers. To form each dumpling, drop a heaping tablespoon of the batter into the simmering stew. When all the batter has been added, cover the pot and cook until a wooden skewer inserted into the center of a dumpling comes out clean, about 15 to 20 minutes. Serve hot, scooping dumplings along with some of the stew into each bowl.

Serves 6.

Cornbread

In numerous cookbooks I've read that southerners only eat white cornbread without any added sweetener and that Yankees only bake yellow cornbread and always add sugar. I don't know which cookbook author began this myth, which has been perpetuated for far too many years. In my native Louisiana our almost-daily cornbread was always yellow and sweetened. In frequent travels throughout the South, I never encountered white cornbread. A recent poll of southern friends and expatriates from North Carolina to East Texas agreed with my experience. So to set the record straight, let me state this: Some residents on each side of the Mason-Dixon line enjoy bread made from yellow cornmeal and others prefer using white or blue; preference is equally divided on whether to add sweetener.

If you enjoy a fine-textured cornbread, choose American fine or regular grind cornmeal. For a coarser-grained bread, use polenta or other coarsely ground meal. If you prefer a dark, crusty exterior, grease an iron pan and preheat it along with the oven while you prepare the batter; then pour the batter into the smoking hot pan.

I've never found a cornbread that I like better than this standard recipe. For the sake of variety, try some of the suggestions on the following two pages.

1 cup cornmeal, preferably freshly stone-ground
1 cup all-purpose flour, preferably unbleached
¼ cup granulated sugar, or ⅓ cup honey (optional)
1 tablespoon baking powder
1 teaspoon salt, or to taste
2 eggs
¼ cup (½ stick) unsalted butter, melted, or safflower or other high-quality vegetable oil
1 cup milk

Preheat an oven to 400° F. Grease a baking pan measuring 8 inches in diameter or 8 inches square.

In a medium-sized bowl, combine the cornmeal, flour, sugar (if using), baking powder, and salt; mix well.

In another bowl, combine the eggs, melted butter or oil, and milk; beat well. Pour the wet ingredients into the dry ingredients and stir just until the mixture is blended. Pour into the prepared pan and bake until golden brown and a wooden skewer inserted in the center comes out clean, about 20 to 25 minutes.

Serves 4 to 6.

ADDITIONS TO BASIC CORNBREAD

Prepare the batter for Cornbread on the preceding page. Stir into the finished batter any one of the following suggestions or a pleasing combination. Bake as directed in basic recipe.

BACON CORNBREAD. Add ½ cup crumbled, crisply fried bacon.

BERRY CORNBREAD. Add 1 cup whole blueberries or raspberries, or 1 cup coarsely chopped cranberries or strawberries.

CHEESE CORNBREAD. Add 1 cup freshly shredded Cheddar or Monterey Jack, crumbled creamy goat's milk or blue cheese, or other good-melting cheese.

CHILE POWDER CORNBREAD. Add 2 tablespoons ground dried hot chile, preferably *ancho* or *pasilla* chile. For a spicier bread, add more chile.

CITRUS CORNBREAD. Add 3 tablespoons freshly minced or grated orange or tangerine zest, or 2 tablespoons freshly minced or grated lemon or lime zest.

CRACKLINGS CORNBREAD. Add ½ cup freshly cooked pork or duck cracklings (pieces of fat fried until fat is liquid and can be separated from crisp connective tissues, which are the cracklings).

CORNBREAD VARIATIONS

Follow directions for basic Cornbread on the preceding page, altering recipe as desired from the following suggestions.

Buttermilk Cornbread. Reduce the baking powder to 1½ teaspoons and add ½ teaspoon baking soda to the dry ingredients. Substitute 1 cup buttermilk for the regular milk. Bake as directed in basic recipe.

Caribbean Cornbread. Add ½ teaspoon *each* ground cinnamon, nutmeg, and cloves to the dry ingredients. Substitute ½ cup *each* heavy (whipping) cream or canned evaporated milk and unsweetened coconut milk for the 1 cup regular milk. Stir in 1 cup finely grated fresh or unsweetened dried (dessicated) coconut. Bake as directed in basic recipe.

Cornbread Fritters. Prepare the basic batter or one of the variations. Thin the batter with about ½ cup milk to the consistency of pancake batter and drop by spoonfuls onto a preheated, lightly greased griddle or skillet. Cook until bubbly on the top, about 3 to 4 minutes, then turn with a spatula and cook the other side until golden, about 3 to 4 minutes longer. Transfer to paper toweling to drain briefly.

Cornbread Muffins. Pour the basic batter or any of the variations into greased muffin tins, filling each well about three fourths full. Bake as directed in basic recipe, but reduce baking time to about 15 minutes.

Cornbread Sticks. Generously grease cornstick molds and preheat in a 450° F oven until smoking hot. Fill each indention about three fourths full with basic batter or any one of the variations and return the pan to the hot oven. Bake until golden, about 10 minutes.

Custard Cornbread. For cornbread with a center of creamy custard, place 2 tablespoons unsalted butter in the baking pan and heat in a 350° F oven until the butter melts. Combine the dry ingredients as described, but reduce the baking powder to 1 teaspoon and add ½ teaspoon baking soda. When mixing the wet ingredients, increase the milk to 2 cups, use melted butter instead of oil, and add 1½ tablespoons distilled white vinegar. Pour the batter into the preheated pan, then pour 1 cup heavy (whipping) cream over the top; do not stir. Bake until lightly browned, about 1 hour.

Extrarich Cornbread. Increase eggs to 3 and increase melted butter to ⅓ cup (do not use oil). Add ¼ cup heavy (whipping) cream along with the milk. Bake as directed in basic recipe.

Flourless Cornbread. For a thin, crunchy cornbread, omit the flour, sugar, and baking powder in basic batter. Increase cornmeal to 2 cups and add 1 teaspoon baking soda to the dry ingredients. Substitute 2 cups buttermilk for the 1 cup regular milk. Bake as directed in basic recipe.

Hush Puppies. Increase cornmeal to 2 cups, reduce flour to ½ cup, and add 1 teaspoon baking soda to the dry ingredients. Substitute 2 cups buttermilk for the 1 cup regular milk and omit the butter or oil. After combining wet and dry ingredients, stir in 5 tablespoons grated white onion or minced green onion (including green top) and, if desired, 2 or 3 minced fresh or canned green hot chiles. Pour peanut or other high-quality vegetable oil into a deep-fat fryer or deep pan to a depth of about 2 inches; preheat to 375° F. Carefully drop the batter, a scant tablespoon at a time, into the hot oil; avoid overcrowding. Turning frequently, fry until crisp and golden, about 5 minutes. Remove with a slotted utensil to paper toweling to drain briefly. Serve hot.

Mexican Cornbread. Preheat an oven to 350° F. Grease a 9- by 13-inch baking pan. Reduce the sugar to 2 tablespoons and substitute ½ cup sour cream for the 1 cup milk. After combining wet and dry ingredients, stir in 2 cups Creamed Fresh Corn (page 14) or 1 can (17 ounces) cream-style corn, 1 cup grated yellow onion, 2 cups (about 12 ounces) freshly shredded Monterey Jack or Cheddar cheese, and 7 or 8 fresh jalapeño or other hot chiles, roasted, peeled, and chopped, or 1 can (4 ounces) jalapeño chiles, drained and chopped. Pour into prepared pan and bake until golden brown and a wooden skewer inserted in the center comes out clean, about 1 hour.

Rice and Corn Bread. Increase eggs to 3 and milk to 1½ cups. Reduce melted butter or oil to 2 tablespoons. After combining wet and dry ingredients, stir in 1 cup cooked rice. Bake as directed in basic recipe.

Sour Cream or Yogurt Cornbread. Substitute 1 cup sour cream or plain low-fat yogurt for the 1 cup milk. Bake as directed in basic recipe.

Whole Wheat Cornbread. Reduce unbleached flour to ½ cup. Add ½ cup whole wheat flour to dry ingredients. Bake as directed in basic recipe.

DOUBLE-CORN CORNBREAD. Add ¾ cup fresh, drained canned, or thawed frozen corn kernels.

HERBED CORNBREAD. Add 2 tablespoons minced fresh or 2 teaspoons crumbled dried dill, rosemary, sage, thyme, or other favorite herb.

NUTTY CORNBREAD. Add ¾ cup chopped pecans or other nuts, preferably toasted.

PEANUT BUTTER CORNBREAD. Add ½ cup crunchy peanut butter.

RED PEPPER CORNBREAD. Use ¼ cup olive oil in place of the butter or oil called for in batter. Sauté ½ cup *each* finely chopped red onion and red sweet pepper in 2 tablespoons olive oil. Add to the batter.

SAUSAGE CORNBREAD. Add 1 pound mild or hot sausage, cooked, well drained, and crumbled.

SEEDED CORNBREAD. Add ½ cup toasted sesame or sunflower seeds, or 3 tablespoons caraway seeds.

VEGETABLE CORNBREAD. Add 1½ cups finely grated carrot or summer squash, or ¾ cup puréed cooked pumpkin or other winter squash.

Smoky Cornbread Dressing

My brother-in-law, John Richardson, created this unique dressing by adapting a Craig Claiborne recipe. John prepares the dressing while a turkey is on the outdoor smoker; about three hours before the turkey is ready, he transfers the bird to the top of the dressing, wraps the pan tightly in foil, and completes the cooking of the turkey in a conventional oven. The smoked fowl imparts a marvelous smoky flavor to the dressing. Heating commercially prepared smoked fowl or meats on the dressing for about an hour accomplishes a similar effect.

The dressing can also be used to stuff a turkey or other fowl. Although it will lack the smoky flavor, the mixture is excellent simply baked in a pan on its own and served alongside roasted or grilled fare.

Preheat an oven to 325° F.

Prepare the cornbread. Cool and finely crumble into a large bowl.

Scatter the bread cubes on a baking sheet and bake until dry and crisp, about 10 minutes. Toss with the crumbled cornbread.

In a sauté pan or skillet, melt the butter over medium-high heat. Add the onion, sweet pepper, and celery and sauté until soft, about 5 minutes. Stir in the sage and garlic and sauté 1 minute longer. Add the liver and sauté just until it loses its raw color. Stir the mixture into the cornbread mixture. Add the grated eggs, raw eggs, and just enough stock or broth to moisten the mixture.

Spread the cornbread mixture in a medium-sized roasting pan and pat down slightly. Add smoked fowl as described in recipe introduction, if desired. Cover tightly with aluminum foil and bake until set, about 3 hours. Serve from the baking dish, or spoon onto a platter, top with pieces of skin removed from the smoked bird, and garnish with herb bouquet.

Serves 8 to 10.

Mexican Cornbread (page 77)
5 slices white or whole wheat bread, cut into small cubes
¼ cup (½ stick) unsalted butter
2½ cups finely chopped yellow onion
1½ cups finely chopped red or green sweet pepper
1½ cups finely chopped celery
2 tablespoons minced fresh sage, or 2 teaspoons crumbled dried sage
2 teaspoons minced or pressed garlic
6 chicken livers, finely chopped
2 hard-cooked eggs, grated
3 raw eggs, lightly beaten
About ½ cup homemade chicken stock or canned chicken broth
Smoked fowl (see recipe introduction; optional)
Fresh herb bouquet, such as parsley, sage, rosemary, and thyme, tied with a whole chive

Double-Corn Spoon Bread

1¾ cups water
¾ cup coarsely ground cornmeal
2 cups (about 6 ounces) freshly
    shredded sharp Cheddar cheese
    or other good-melting cheese
¼ cup (½ stick) unsalted butter,
    softened
½ teaspoon salt, or to taste
Freshly ground black pepper
1 cup buttermilk
4 eggs, separated
¾ cup fresh, drained canned, or
    thawed frozen corn kernels

An Early American favorite, soft cornbread served with a spoon is a hearty dish for breakfast, lunch, or supper. Use yellow kernels and cornmeal with yellow-tinted Cheddar for a golden version, or combine white corn, cornmeal, and natural cream-colored cheese for a white spoon bread. For a more unusual presentation, start with blue cornmeal and add white kernels and good-quality blue cheese.

Preheat an oven to 350° F. Grease a 2-quart soufflé dish or ovenproof casserole.

In a medium-sized saucepan, combine the water and cornmeal; stir well. Place over low heat and cook, stirring frequently and scraping the bottom of the pan with a wooden spoon, until cornmeal is smooth and thick, about 10 minutes.

Remove cornmeal from the heat; add cheese, butter, salt, and pepper to taste. Stir until the cheese melts. Gradually pour in the buttermilk, stirring constantly. In a small bowl, lightly beat the egg yolks. Stir them into the cornmeal mixture along with the corn kernels.

In a separate bowl, beat the egg whites with a wire whisk or electric beater until stiff peaks form. Stir about 2 tablespoons of the egg whites into the cornmeal mixture to lighten it, then gently fold in the remaining whites. Pour the batter into the prepared dish and bake until firm and golden brown, about 50 to 55 minutes. Serve piping hot.

Serves 6.

VARIATIONS Before folding in the egg whites, add any one or a pleasing combination of the following: ¾ cup crumbled, crisply cooked bacon, ¾ cup chopped, toasted pecans or other nuts, 2 to 3 tablespoons minced fresh herbs or 2 to 3 teaspoons crumbled dried herbs, ground cayenne or other dried ground hot chile to taste, ½ cup sautéed, minced red sweet pepper, ¾ cup toasted sesame or sunflower seeds.

Buttermilk Corn Cakes
with Spicy Crab Butter

For this tasty first course, choose white, yellow, or blue cornmeal. Corn kernels in both the batter and the butter add extra crunchiness.

To make the crab butter, melt the butter in a small saucepan. Remove from heat and stir in lime or lemon juice and chile. Let stand at room temperature for about 15 minutes. Reserve the remaining crab butter ingredients.

To make the corn cakes, combine the cornmeal, flour, baking soda, sugar, and salt in a medium-sized bowl.

In a small bowl, combine the butter or oil, buttermilk, and egg. Stir well, then quickly mix the wet ingredients into the dry ingredients. Stir in the 3 tablespoons minced chives or green onion and corn. Let stand for 10 minutes to soften the cornmeal.

Preheat a griddle or large, heavy skillet and preheat an oven to 200° F.

Lightly grease the hot griddle. Using about ¼ cup batter for each cake, pour the batter on the griddle. Cook until tops of cakes are bubbly, about 3 to 4 minutes. Turn cakes with a spatula and cook until golden on the other side, about 3 to 4 minutes longer. Transfer each batch of pancakes to a plate and keep warm in the oven until all the pancakes are cooked.

Just before serving, heat the reserved butter mixture in a sauté pan or skillet over medium-high heat. Add the crab meat and the corn and sauté until the corn is cooked, about 5 minutes. Season to taste with salt.

To serve, arrange the pancakes on individual plates. Top with the crab butter, sprinkle with minced chives or green onion, and serve immediately.

Serves 4 to 6.

BREAKFAST VARIATION Omit the Spicy Crab Butter, chives or green onions, and fresh corn kernels. As soon as the pancakes are on the griddle, sprinkle each cake with fresh blueberries. Pass melted butter and warm maple syrup.

SPICY CRAB BUTTER
½ cup (1 stick) unsalted butter
2 tablespoons freshly squeezed lime or lemon juice
2 teaspoons ground cayenne or other ground dried hot chile, or to taste
½ pound cooked crab meat, picked over and chopped or shredded
1 cup fresh, drained canned, or thawed frozen corn kernels
Salt

CORN CAKES
1½ cups cornmeal, preferably coarse or stone-ground
¼ cup all-purpose flour
1 teaspoon baking soda
2 teaspoons granulated sugar
½ teaspoon salt
2 tablespoons unsalted butter, melted, or safflower or other high-quality vegetable oil
1⅔ cups buttermilk
1 egg, lightly beaten
3 tablespoons minced fresh chives or green onion, including green top
1 cup fresh, drained canned, or thawed frozen corn kernels
Minced fresh chives or green onion, including green top, for sprinkling on top

Maple Popcorn

1 cup popcorn kernels
¾ cup melted unsalted butter
1½ cups pure maple syrup
½ cup light corn syrup
1 teaspoon salt
¼ teaspoon cream of tartar
½ teaspoon baking soda

Mary McCoy, to whom this book is dedicated, loves maple syrup almost as much as she does corn. She introduced me to this Vermont tradition that combines two of her favorite foods. Although the recipe should serve six, I must admit that the first time I made it was during a terrific electric storm over Lake Tahoe, and I devoured the entire batch in one afternoon while watching nature's spectacular light show.

For savory flavored popcorns, see page 51.

Pop the popcorn according to your favorite method (page 50) and distribute equally between two 9- by 13-inch ovenproof pans.

Preheat an oven to 200° F.

In a large saucepan, melt the butter over medium-high heat. Add the maple and corn syrups, salt, and cream of tartar and mix well. Cook, without stirring, until a candy thermometer inserted in the mixture registers 240° F, or a spoonful of the syrup forms a soft, pliable ball when dropped in cold water. Remove from the heat and stir in baking soda.

Pour the syrup over the popcorn and stir to coat thoroughly. Bake, stirring several times, for 1 hour. Cool completely before serving. To store, place in a tightly covered container.

Serves 6.

VARIATION Replace about 1 cup of the popped corn with an equal amount of roasted peanuts or coarsely chopped, toasted pecans or other nuts.

From James

Twice-Baked Cornmeal Cookies
(Biscotti di Polenta)

These little nuggets are great on their own or for dunking in coffee, hot chocolate, or fruity wine.

Preheat an oven to 400° F. Lightly butter and flour a baking sheet.

In a medium-sized bowl, combine the flour, cornmeal, sugar, baking powder, salt, eggs, and almond extract; beat until the dough is smooth. Stir in the nuts. Gather up the dough with fingers and form into a ball; cut ball into 4 equal portions. The dough will be quite soft and sticky.

Dust a work surface well with flour. With flour-dusted palms, place each piece of dough on work surface and roll into a rope about 9 inches long and about 2½ inches in diameter; as you roll, incorporate flour as needed to keep dough from sticking to surface. Place the finished ropes several inches apart on the prepared baking sheet. Flatten tops slightly with fingers so that the sides of each rope are a little flatter than the center. Brush the exposed surface of each piece of dough evenly with the glaze mixture and bake until golden, about 20 minutes.

Remove from the oven and cool about 5 minutes, then cut each cookie loaf crosswise into slices about 1 inch thick. Arrange the pieces on an ungreased baking sheet and return to the oven until dry, about 5 minutes longer. Transfer to a wire rack to cool completely. Store in airtight containers.

Makes about 3 dozen cookies.

1⅓ cups all-purpose flour, preferably unbleached
1 cup yellow cornmeal
¾ cup granulated sugar
1½ teaspoons baking powder
¼ teaspoon salt
3 eggs, beaten
1 teaspoon almond extract
⅔ cup (about 4 ounces) finely chopped almonds or other nuts
1 egg yolk mixed with 1 tablespoon milk for glaze

Indian Pudding with Caramel Custard Sauce (Cajeta)

INDIAN PUDDING

½ cup cornmeal
4 cups cold milk
1 cup firmly packed dark brown sugar
½ cup unsulphured molasses
6 tablespoons (¾ stick) unsalted
    butter, melted
1 tablespoon ground ginger
1 teaspoon freshly grated nutmeg
1½ teaspoons salt
1 cup light cream or half-and-half,
    heated almost to boiling point

CARAMEL CUSTARD SAUCE

2 cans (14 ounces *each*) evaporated
    milk, preferably goat's milk
2 cans (12 ounces *each*) sweetened
    condensed milk
6 tablespoons (¾ stick) unsalted
    butter

Introduced by native Americans to the English who settled along the northeastern seaboard, this traditional sweet is teamed with a sauce from the Southwest. The sauce is traditionally made from canned milk, a holdover from the days when fresh milk was a rarity in the arid terrain.

The pudding is also delicious served with a scoop of vanilla ice cream or softly whipped cream in place of the sauce.

To make the pudding, preheat an oven to 350° F. Grease a 2-quart baking dish.

In a heavy saucepan, combine the cornmeal and milk; stir well. Place over medium-high heat and bring to a simmer, stirring occasionally with a wooden spoon. Reduce the heat to low and simmer, stirring frequently and scraping the bottom of the pan with the spoon, until thick and smooth, about 10 minutes. Remove from the heat and stir in the sugar, molasses, butter, ginger, nutmeg, and salt. Pour into the prepared baking dish. Place baking dish in a large baking pan and pour hot water into baking pan to reach halfway up side of pudding dish. Bake until bubbly, about 30 minutes.

Pour the heated light cream evenly over the top of the pudding and continue baking until set to the touch, about 2 hours longer.

To make the sauce, combine the milks and butter in a saucepan over medium-high heat and bring to a boil. Cook, stirring quite frequently, for 10 minutes. Reduce the heat to medium-low and cook, stirring constantly, until the sauce thickens and is a medium tan color, about 5 minutes longer. Serve immediately, or cool to room temperature, cover, and refrigerate for up to 2 weeks. Reheat in a microwave oven, stirring several times, or in a saucepan over low heat, stirring almost continuously, until smooth and warm; stir in a little milk or cream if the mixture is too thick.

Serve the warm pudding with the warm sauce.

Serves 6.

White Corn Cake with White Chocolate Frosting

WHITE CORN CAKE

1 cup finely ground white cornmeal
1 cup white cake flour
¼ teaspoon salt
1 cup (2 sticks) unsalted butter, softened
1½ cups granulated sugar
4 egg whites
2 teaspoons pure vanilla extract
2 cups Creamed Fresh Corn (page 14), made with white corn kernels

WHITE CHOCOLATE FROSTING

1 pound high-quality white chocolate, finely chopped
1½ cups heavy (whipping) cream
1 tablespoon pure vanilla extract
Crushed ice
½ cup very finely chopped pistachios

Canned creamed white corn can be substituted for the freshly made version in this unusual confection. For a yellow cake, use creamed yellow corn, yellow cornmeal, and whole eggs. Substitute dark or milk chocolate for the white chocolate in the frosting.

Preheat an oven to 325° F. Butter and flour two 8-inch round cake pans or one 9-inch bundt pan, preferably with a nonstick surface.

To make the cake, sift together the cornmeal, flour, and salt into a bowl; mix well.

Place the butter in a large bowl and beat until creamy and smooth. Add the sugar and beat until well blended. Add the egg whites, one at a time, and beat thoroughly after each addition. Stir in the vanilla and creamed corn. Stir the dry ingredients into the wet ingredients and mix until blended. Spoon into the prepared pans, smooth top, and bake until a wooden skewer inserted in the center comes out clean, about 35 minutes for the 2 layers, about 55 minutes for the bundt cake. Cover cake with aluminum foil if top begins to brown too much during baking.

Remove pans to wire racks to cool for about 5 minutes. Turn cake(s) out onto racks to cool completely.

To make the frosting, place the chocolate and cream in a bowl and microwave, stirring frequently, until melted, about 2 minutes. Alternatively, place the chocolate and cream in the top pan of a double boiler set over barely simmering water. Stir gently until chocolate melts. Transfer the melted chocolate mixture to a bowl, stir in the vanilla, and set inside a larger bowl filled with ice. Whisk or beat until spreadable.

Position one layer of the cake on a plate and spread with frosting. Cover with the remaining layer and spread the frosting over the top and sides. Or place the bundt cake on a plate and cover completely with the frosting. Sprinkle frosted cake with the pistachios.

Serves 8 to 10.

Red Chile Sauce

12 dried whole *ancho*, *pasilla*, or
  other dried hot chiles, one kind
  or an assortment
½ pound ripe tomatoes, or ½ cup
  seeded, chopped, and well-
  drained canned plum tomatoes
2 tablespoons olive oil
1 cup coarsely chopped yellow onion
4 garlic cloves
1 teaspoon dried whole-leaf oregano
2 cups water, homemade beef,
  chicken, or pork stock, or
  canned beef or chicken broth
Salt

My version of this New Mexico staple has a hint of tomato to cool the fiery chiles. It is excellent with tamales, tostadas, enchiladas, and other southwestern and Mexican dishes. It is also marvelous stirred into or spooned over polenta.

Dried chiles are available in Mexican groceries, ethnic sections of supermarkets, or natural-foods stores. An assortment of chiles creates a more complex flavor. For a heartier sauce, cut two pounds boneless beef, pork, or chicken into small bite-sized pieces and add to the simmering sauce; cook until the meat is tender.

Preheat an oven to 400° F.

Rinse the chiles well under cold running water to remove dust. Shake off excess water and lay the chiles on a baking sheet. Roast in the oven until lightly toasted, about 4 minutes; do not burn. Cool slightly, then discard stems; split the chiles open and discard seeds and membranes. Reserve chiles.

If using fresh tomatoes, position them over a gas flame, on a charcoal grill, or under a preheated broiler and turn frequently until the skin is charred. Cool for 5 minutes, then pull off blackened skin. Split tomatoes and discard seeds. Reserve tomatoes.

In a saucepan over medium-high heat, heat the oil. Add the onion and sauté until soft, about 5 minutes. Stir in garlic and oregano and sauté 1 minute longer. Add reserved chiles and water, stock, or broth. Bring to a boil over high heat, reduce the heat to low, cover, and simmer until the chiles are very tender, about 30 minutes.

Transfer chile mixture to a food processor or blender. Add reserved tomatoes and purée until smooth. Season to taste with salt. Rub purée through a fine wire sieve into a bowl. Transfer to a saucepan and cook over medium heat until slightly thickened, about 10 minutes. Reheat just before serving.

Makes about 2 cups.

Black Bean Sauce

Overnight soaking is unnecessary for the newer strains of black beans now on the market. If those strains are unavailable, soak the beans overnight in cold water to cover; drain beans the next day and proceed as directed.

Carefully pick over the beans to remove any shriveled beans and foreign matter. Rinse well under running cold water; reserve.

Heat the oil in a deep pan over medium-high heat. Add the onion and chile and sauté until soft, about 5 minutes. Add the garlic, oregano, thyme, cumin, and coriander and sauté 1 minute longer. Add the beans, bay leaves, and stock, water, or diluted broth. Bring to a boil, then reduce heat, cover, and simmer 1½ hours.

Stir the tomato purée into the beans and season to taste with salt and pepper. Cover and simmer until the beans begin to fall apart, about 1½ hours longer; add more liquid if necessary to keep beans covered during cooking.

Working in batches, transfer the beans and their liquid to a food processor or blender and purée, adding extra stock, water, or diluted broth if needed to make a fairly smooth purée. For a blacker sauce, stir in Kitchen Bouquet and food coloring until the mixture reaches the desired color. Serve warm, or cool, cover, and refrigerate; reheat gently before serving.

Makes about 2 cups.

WHITE BEAN VARIATION Use any dried white beans such as cannellini, Great Northern, or navy. After picking over the beans, cover them with cold water, soak overnight, and drain. Proceed as directed in the recipe, but omit tomato purée. For a whiter sauce, drain beans before puréeing and thin with light or heavy (whipping) cream as needed to make a fairly smooth sauce.

1 cup dried black (turtle) beans
2 tablespoons olive oil
½ cup chopped yellow onion
2 teaspoons chopped fresh or canned jalapeño or other hot chile, or to taste
1 teaspoon minced or pressed garlic
2 teaspoons minced fresh oregano, or 1 teaspoon crumbled dried oregano
2 teaspoons minced fresh thyme, or 1 teaspoon crumbled dried thyme
¾ teaspoon ground cumin
½ teaspoon ground coriander
2 bay leaves
5 cups homemade light chicken stock or water, or 2½ cups canned chicken broth mixed with 2½ cups water
¼ cup tomato purée
Salt
Freshly ground black pepper
Kitchen Bouquet (optional)
1 part red to 2 parts blue liquid food coloring (optional)

Index

Recipe Index

ACKNOWLEDGMENTS

To Bill LeBlond, my editor, for giving me a little extra time to complete this book after a bout in Santa Fe with the Shanghai flu. And to the staff of Chronicle Books, who perform countless tasks in the printing, distribution, and promotion of my book series.

To those who shared both recipes and ideas that became recipes: Eula Cain, Victoria Flores, Mary King, Mary McCoy, Lucille McNair, Jack Porter, Marilyn "Babs" Retzer, John Richardson, Socoro Sandavol, and Betty Wood.

To Sharon Silva for her excellent copy editing and food expertise.

To Michael Léson for the plates shown on pages 82 and 91.

To my assistant, Ellen Berger-Quan, for her diligent research, recipe testing, creative ideas, innovative shopping, and exuberant work in both the office and kitchen.

To Cleve Gallat and his CTA Graphics staff for another superb round of typography and mechanical production.

To Patricia Brabant for her talented eye that makes our collaborative efforts so successful. And to her assistant, M. J. Murphy, for keeping us on track and sustaining us with tea and practical jokes.

To my sister, Martha McNair, for her magical assistance in the studio.

To my family and friends who are always there for me.

To my loyal companions, Addie Prey, Buster Booroo, Michael T. Wigglebutt, Joshua J. Chew, and Dweasel Pickle, who all love cornbread.

To my partner, Lin Cotton, for his constant support and guidance.